CRIMES OF PASSION
THAT SHOCKED
AUSTRALIA

Published by Brolga Publishing Pty Ltd
ABN 46 063 962 443
PO Box 12544, A'Beckett St, VIC, 8006, Australia
email: markzocchi@brolgapublishing.com.au

National Library of Australia Cataloguing-in-Publication entry

       Crimes of passion that shocked Australia : and other crimes
       / Ian Ferguson ; Paul Bugeja.
       1st ed.
       9781921596339 (pbk.)
       Includes index.
       Bibliography.
       Violent crimes—Australia—Case studies.
       Crime—Australia—History.
       Crime—Australia—Case studies.
       Criminals—Australia—History.
       364.10994

Printed in Hong Kong
Cover by David Khan
Design and typeset by Imogen Stubbs

CRIMES OF PASSION THAT SHOCKED AUSTRALIA
AND OTHER CRIMES

IAN FERGUSON
AND PAUL BUGEJA

CONTENTS

My heartfelt thanks go once more to my wife
Ann for her valued support and proofreading skills.

Ian Ferguson

• • •

This, the first, must go to Per.
Your presence in my life gave me the
nudge to get on with the 'write' stuff.
Thanks.

Paul Bugeja

FOREWORD

Three passions, simple but overwhelmingly strong,
have governed my life:
The longing for love,
The search for knowledge,
And unbearable pity for the suffering of mankind.
These passions, like great winds, have blown me hither
and thither, in a wayward course, over a great ocean of
anguish, reaching to the very verge of despair.

Bertrand Russell

When Bertrand Russell, one of the great philosophers of modern times, voiced these words of wisdom in the prologue to his autobiography, it would be fair to say he managed to encapsulate three of humanities greatest drivers of passion.

Of the three, many would argue that love, by a long stretch, holds first place, as it is so carefully and intricately

1

woven into many aspects of our lives.

Religion (theoretically) has love at its core and the formalised outcome of love, marriage, is a legislated institution, providing many benefits and a sense of belonging to those who subscribe to it. Products are marketed around love and we even have a day set aside to celebrate it—Valentine's Day. Every Hollywood movie contains love, no matter what the genre, every second song to hit the airwaves croons of it and romantic fiction is the biggest seller in bookstores the world over.

We cannot escape love

We cannot escape love and, more importantly, we will often go to any length to keep it in our lives, which unfortunately brings with it love's counterpoint—tragedy.

Think about some of the great lovers throughout history, real or imagined.

The Old Testament's Samson and Delilah.

Shakespeare's Romeo and Juliet.

The British Monarchy's Queen Victoria and Prince Albert.

Rose and Jack from the blockbuster *The Titanic*.

Ennis and Jack from Annie Proux's modern classic, *Brokeback Mountain*.

For all these lovers, despite their passion, tragedy oozed from their relationships, and love was a veritable battlefield with mine's aplenty, exploding drama and misfortune at every step.

Love, for all the wonder that it promised, was dragging them inexorably towards some kind of calamity or another.

In extreme cases, love can become so all consuming and overpowering that if there is any indication of it being denied, or if it has a negative effect of some kind, the desire to take some action to prevent such overrides the love itself.

All it takes is a moment where the passion that originally came with the love—which drove and pushed the love to the highest of heights—curdles as the lover realises he or she cannot have what they want...

In a split second, jealousy, revenge, and lust can lead to murder.

In a split second, jealousy, revenge, and lust can lead to murder.

•   •   •

This extreme form of love has led to what are commonly referred to as 'crimes of passion'.

In common understanding, these crimes are incidents in which the perpetrator commits a crime, most often assault or murder, against a loved one because of a sudden strong impulse such as jealousy, rage or heartbreak. There is little or no premeditation—everything happens in an 'out of control' moment, and often the consequences are of the worst kind.

In the United States, a crime of passion is

referred to as temporary insanity and was first used a defence by a US Congressman in 1859 after he had killed his wife's lover, going on to be used often in the 1940s and '50s.

Other countries, notably France, until recent times had the *crime passionnel as* a valid defence during murder cases—during the 19th century, some cases could be a mere custodial sentence for the murderer, while the ill-fated spouse's sentence was their death at the hands of their spouse. This ended in France in the 1970s when the Napoleonic Code was updated so that a specific father's authority upon his whole family was finally terminated—not that this stopped such crimes being committed!

...the ill-fated spouse's sentence was their death at the hands of their spouse.

Australia has undoubtedly seen its fair share of crimes of passion.

Let's not forget, we started out as a convict colony. Ships, laden with all the worst of Britain's wrongdoers, came to our shores holding their fair share of men and women convicted for crimes of passion, sentenced to the new colony for the terms of their natural lives. In addition, as early as fifty or so years after settlement, one of our first recorded crimes of passion came before the courts in the case of Bridget Hurford (Section One, Chapter 1).

● ● ●

Crimes of Passion that Shocked Australia, as the title suggests, goes beyond the normal brief that a book on crimes of passion normally adhere to.

Section One, *Traditional Crimes of Passion*, deals predominantly with crimes that snugly fit into the conventional view and definition of a crime of passion. Section Two takes a look at crimes that remain *Unsolved or Unproven* or where the prosecuted maintains their *Innocence*, in some cases all the way to their death. Section Three considers the notion of *Provocation*, long used as a defence for certain crimes of passion, but slowly being removed from most jurisdictions or radically altered to ensure crimes are justly punished. Unfortunately, it has taken the deaths of several people, all women, for this to occur.

From Section Four onwards, the book departs from stereotypical crimes of passion to examine various other chilling crimes that mimic crimes of passion or involve some substantial degree of passion in their undertaking:

- Section Four deals with *Family Affairs,* where a family member commits a crime, most usually murder, within their own family
- Section Five covers *Random Crimes of Passion* where one or more perpetrators have

committed a crime that is evocative of a crime of passion

- Section Six, *Stand by your Man*, studies some of our more infamous women criminals or associates of criminals, and the roles they have played in crimes committed for loved ones, often driven by their passion for partners or family
- Section Seven, *Pushed over the Edge: Our Mass Murderers*, is on the surface the most substantial departure in this book from traditional crimes of passion, which in the main do not involve multiple murders. However, two Australian mass murderers in particular committed their crimes in such a way that a parallel may be drawn to crimes of passion

... it can also lead men and women down dark and desperate ways— destination, death.

So, read on, and immerse yourself in the lives and minds of some of Australia's worst criminals, driven to their crimes by all-consuming passion.

The more you read, the more it will become patently clear that while love may be 'a many splendored thing', given the passion it so often evokes, it can also lead men and women down dark and desperate ways— destination, death.

Paul Bugeja, January 2010

SECTION ONE:

TRADITIONAL CRIMES
OF PASSION

*"There are crimes of passion
and crimes of logic.
The boundary between them
is not clearly defined."*

Albert Camus

Traditional crimes of passion have long been an identifiable sub-class of crime, or more particularly, a way of classifying murders and lesser crimes of manslaughter.

They occur at every level of society—rich or poor, believer or atheist, male or female, young or old, straight or gay.

Crimes of passion also nearly always, unfortunately, involve the death of one person at the hands of another who is supposed to love them, or who will stop at nothing to have the object of their affection in their life.

CHAPTER 1

CRIMES FROM THE PAST (1850s-1980s)

WILD WILD WEST

John Hurford's much younger wife, Bridget Hurford, created history in Western Australia in 1855, albeit in a way she would never fully appreciate.

Hurford's farming, whaling and timber business interests had prospered by the time he reached the age of 65. He surprised many when, in 1851, he married a widow 30 years his junior—Bridget Hurford, nee Larkin—who brought six children along into her new marriage following the drowning death of her husband four years prior.

April 1855 saw John leave his own home to take up residence in a neighbour's house after reporting to friends he had suffered physical abuse at the hands of his wife. However, with some reluctance, he returned home when the neighbour's residence became too crowded.

Within a month of his return, the aging Hurford fell ill and suddenly died. Despite some minor red marks around his neck, something the doctor placed little significance upon, 'natural causes' was declared as the cause of death at the inquest.

Had it not been for Enoch Dodd, the matter might have ended there.

Employed as a labourer on the property, Dodd and Bridget had commenced an adulterous relationship before her husband's death, which proved just as tempestuous as her marital one.

When a drunken Dodd confessed to Phillip Dixon, another farmhand, he had battered John Hurford before strangling him to death, he also confided that Bridget had paid him one hundred pounds and presented him with her late husband's horse in reward for the murder. He swore Dixon to secrecy, something he thought he could do given Dixon's hand in forging Hurford's will.

Unfortunately for Dodd, Dixon could not hold his tongue.

When information about the homicide reached Governor Kennedy, he had the couple arrested. Although evidence presented in court was largely circumstantial, and the court deemed void the accounts of the doctor at the inquest when it was discovered he had not passed a professional medical examination, both Hurford and Dodd were found guilty of murder.

...presented him with her late husband's horse in reward for the murder.

Bridget Hurford believed authorities would not hang a woman, but her optimism was purely speculative—on 15 October 1855, she took on the dubious and infamous title of the first woman to be legally hung in Western Australia.

...the first woman to be legally hung in Western Australia.

THE PYJAMA GIRL

...discovered the badly burnt body of a woman in a culvert...

On the first day of spring in 1934, a young farmer, Tom Griffiths, discovered the badly burnt body of a woman in a culvert on the little used Albury-to-Howlong Road near the NSW and Victorian border.

When police arrived, initial investigations revealed a bullet wound near the victim's right eye, but given how terribly burnt the corpse was, identification was near impossible. A charred towel and bag partly covered her—nearby the police found distinctive green and cream pyjamas with a striking dragon motif on the jacket. They believed the deceased was in her 20s, in good health, had certain notable facial features and had recently undergone extensive dental work. The exotic pyjamas, police predicted, would rapidly lead to identification of the victim, a confidence that proved illusory.

After the initial investigation failed to identify the body, it was taken to Sydney where it was placed on public exhibition and, despite large groups of curious observers viewing it, none was able to shed further light on the identity of 'the pyjama girl'. Unbowed, the police preserved the body in a bath of formalin at the Sydney University Medical School (where it remained until 1942, before being transferred to police headquarters) in the hope they would sometime solve the case.

A year after the initial discovery of the body, the name Linda Agostini (nee Platt) began to surface. Tony Agostini, Linda's Italian-born husband, was located in Melbourne. Police interviewed him, but he convinced them the photograph of the corpse was not his wife. Furthermore, he asserted he had lost touch with her after she left him and apparently became a hairdresser on a cruise ship.

Linda Agostini

Eventually, in January 1938, an Albury inquest brought down its findings—an unknown woman had died from injuries to the skull and brain, inflicted by a person or persons unknown.

...he convinced them the photograph of the corpse was not his wife.

Despite this official case-closure, the public remained fascinated, particularly as new developments continued to surface. Dr. T.A. Palmer Benbow posited that the dead woman was Anna Morgan, a claim also believed by the missing woman's mother. Mrs. Morgan demanded that the preserved corpse become her property, but police remained sceptical about the claims, refusing her request.

A decade on from the body's discovery, the case was suddenly reopened.

On 4 March 1944, William John McKay, then NSW police commissioner, interviewed Tony Agostini, who had relocated to Sydney where he had become a waiter. McKay, a regular patron at *Romano's*, the fashionable restaurant where Tony worked, managed to pry a confession from him.

Agostini went on to tell police he first met Linda Platt in Australia, with them later marrying in her home country of England. After returning to Melbourne, their marriage had rapidly deteriorated due to her excessive drinking, but the couple stayed together.

One Sunday evening, Tony had invited his wife to accompany him the next day on a business trip to Shepparton. She declined, allegedly adding in a threatening tone,

'You will never go to Shepparton.'

This obscure threat troubled him, but the situation became more dangerous shortly after he awoke at 7am when he found Linda allegedly pressing a gun to the back of his head.

In the ensuing struggle, the gun discharged and Tony Agostini discovered, to his horror, his wife was dead from a gunshot wound. After dousing the corpse with petrol and setting it alight in order to lessen the chances of identification, he decided to dispose of her body close to a remote country road near Howlong.

...dousing the corpse with petrol and setting it alight...

On his return to Melbourne, a contrite Tony Agostini confessed his crime to a friend who persuaded him to keep the whole episode a secret.

After police concluded their second interview with Agostini, they charged him with his wife's murder. Returned to Melbourne for his trial, he informed the court that the woman died from the accidental gunshot wound and that the abrasions and bruises later found on her body were sustained after he dropped the heavy corpse against a flat iron as he was attempting to carry it from their house. This explanation produced much debate in the courtroom and the jury apparently became more persuaded than the judge, Sir Charles Low, about Agostini's evidence.

'I think the jury was merciful to you,' Low drolly remarked, when the jury found the defendant guilty of manslaughter rather than murder, and sentenced him to six years of hard labour.

...sentenced him to six years of hard labour.

Following the verdict, Agostini only served three years and nine months of his sentence before authorities deported him to Italy in 1948.

He lived there, in Sardinia, until his death in 1969.

'RATS' ON THE RIVER

In 1964, Leith and Beverly Ratten moved to the Victorian Murray River town of Echuca, where Leith took up work as a surveyor. The young couple soon became friends with Peter and Jenny Kemp, reinforced by the men sharing a common love of shooting and fishing.

Not long after, both couples celebrated the arrival of additions to their families and Peter Kemp became a sporting goods salesperson in nearby Barham. The new occupation often took him away from home and Leith Ratten began to drop in on the lonely Jenny when on shooting expeditions to the Barham area. By April 1969, the pair had commenced an affair, even though Beverly Ratten was pregnant with her fourth child.

Ratten soon appeared to be a nervous partner in the extra-marital affair.

Ratten soon appeared to be a nervous partner in the extra-marital affair.

He unsuccessfully applied for various positions in a proposed 1970 Antarctic expedition that would have resulted in a 12-month commitment far away from his problems at home. Jenny Kemp and he allegedly discussed divorcing their respective spouses around this time, going so far as to approach a solicitor in May 1970.

It seems beyond doubt that Jenny Kemp did discuss divorce proceedings with her husband at this time and believed her lover would separate from his wife after their fourth child was born. However, Beverly Ratten gave no indication to her family and friends she knew anything about the affair, and Leith Ratten later claimed he never discussed the matter with his wife, and that he did not intend to leave her.

On 7 May 1970, the Rattens were in their kitchen, where Leith was cleaning a gun. Echuca telephonist Janet Flowers later recalled a high-pitched female voice asking for urgent attendance at 59 Mitchell Street, and when police arrived, a sobbing four-year-old Wendy Ratten was waiting outside the house.

After her father ushered them inside, they discovered the body of Beverly Ratten on the kitchen floor, a shotgun beside her. Both she and her unborn baby were dead, with her apparently distressed husband claiming the gun had accidentally discharged while his wife was making a cup of coffee.

...the gun had accidentally discharged while his wife was making a cup of coffee.

Jenny Kemp admitted her involvement in a sexual relationship to police, but adamantly declared her lover would be incapable of murdering his wife. Her support did not prevent the homicide squad taking over the investigation.

Ratten steadfastly maintained the shooting was accidental. His account, however,

...it was not his wife who had made the distress call to the telephone exchange the day she died.

appeared to be at odds with the point of entry of the fatal bullet, as was his account of his wife's awareness of his extramarital affair when compared to Jenny Kemp's views. She believed Beverly Ratten's strong religious beliefs were the main problem in gaining a divorce settlement, but her lover continued to claim he was not planning to leave his wife.

Ratten further maintained it was not his wife who had made the distress call to the telephone exchange the day she died. Regardless, at the completion of the investigation, Leith Ratten was charged with the murder of his wife and court proceedings began in Shepparton on 10 August 1970.

The Crown Prosecution made much in court of Ratten's unfaithful behaviour, and his deceit to both his wife and his mistress. Despite the fact that there were no witnesses to the shooting, and that much of the evidence presented was circumstantial in nature, a jury found Ratten guilty of murder, sentencing him to 25 years imprisonment.

Following the case, there were four separate appeals on a variety of grounds, one of which required the exhumation of Beverley Ratten's body in 1973. All were dismissed. The case also attracted the interest of an author, writer-lawyer Tom Mollomby, who presented a comprehensive analysis of the evidence in his book, *Ratten: The Web of Circumstances*, possibly pointing to Ratten's innocence.

Eight years later, incoming Victorian Premier John Cain ordered a re-examination of the case, but this attempt failed to provide any compelling new evidence and the original court decision was upheld.

A model prisoner, Leith Ratten finally served the end of his sentence in a minimum-security prison and then moved to Queensland to work as a surveyor.

Eight years later, incoming Victorian Premier John Cain ordered a re-examination of the case...

SISTER ACT

On 12 May 1981, James Mitchell's wife discovered the corpse of her 51-year-old husband near their bed.

He had suffered deep knife wounds to the chest and the examining doctor concluded an assailant had savagely stabbed him before his body had rolled off the bed and onto the floor. Initial police investigations focussed on Mitchell's 31-year-old wife, Pauline, but early evidence indicated she was a model citizen. Both she and her much younger sister, Barbara, were raised in a stable and happy home, and after Pauline married she showed all signs of being a devoted wife.

Consequently, the motive of robbery became the focus.

Strong circumstantial evidence soon linked a young man Mitchell had previously employed in one of his garages to the homicide—when it became evident the man had illegally used a customer's car, Mitchell had terminated his employment.

Just as the case against this disgruntled ex-employee appeared to be strengthening, sensational new evidence was unearthed, dramatically altering the course of the investigation.

This breakthrough came in the form of a letter delivered to an investigating detective,

...an assailant had savagely stabbed him before his body had rolled off the bed...

supposedly penned by a 'Mrs. Joan Handley'. The writer claimed her husband, Peter Handley, had recently renewed a sexual relationship with a certain Pauline Mitchell. The affair had originally begun years before, resulting in the then 16-year-old Pauline Hewitt giving birth to a baby.

A girl, in fact.

Detectives soon realised that 14-year-old Barbara Hewitt was possibly Pauline's daughter, rather than her sister and, following intense questioning, Hewitt and Handley admitted this startling revelation was indeed true.

Each blamed the other for the planned slaying of James Mitchell, but a jury found both guilty of murder in the trial that concluded on 27 July 1981.

The affair had originally begun years before, resulting in the then 16-year-old giving birth to a baby.

TUSSLING WITH DEMONS

David Schwarz

The psychological effects on a witness to a violent homicide are wide and varied, easily overlooked by the victim, and can continue to resonate for years, if not decades, to come.

It was 1981, and David Schwarz, who would later go on to play as an AFL champion for the Melbourne Demons and become fondly known as 'The Ox', was going through the difficult time of his parents recently separating. During the school holidays, eight-year-old Schwarz visited Bright on an access visit to his 31-year-old father, Heinz Schwarz, a chef in the popular tourist town.

David revelled in the opportunity to spend time with his dad. He enjoyed games of pool with him at the Mt. Beauty Club and was looking forward to a fishing trip planned for the next day.

Instead, brutal mayhem intervened.

At 5.30 am, a man in black 'dressed like an army guy' and carrying a .22 gauge rifle broke into the room David was sharing with his father and his father's new partner. The young boy awoke to the frightening sound of a shot fired centimetres above his head. As he arose, he remembers seeing blood everywhere and his father's girlfriend on the ground, struggling with the attacker, who police later identi-

...he remembers seeing blood everywhere and his father's girlfriend on the ground...

fied as her 51-year-old estranged husband.

The terrified boy scrambled to safety through the room's breakfast chute and began banging on the motel manager's door. From the safety of the manager's quarters, Schwarz later learned that the assailant, Richard Martin, had fatally shot his father before turning the weapon on himself.

In later years, Schwarz would go on to play 173 games with the Demons, and was much admired for his talent, ability to overcome serious injury and outgoing personality. Although presented with the opportunity to see psychologists at the club during his time there, he never believed it necessary in relation to his bloodied past.

After retiring from the game, with the support of his partner Karen and psychotherapist Jan Beames he began to confront his own personal 'demons', which presented themselves externally in the form of an addiction to smoking, drinking and gambling. Counselling sessions with Beames soon opened Schwarz up to realising the impact his father's violent death may have had upon him, and Schwarz realised he would not want his own son Cooper to face the traumas foisted on him without the aid of professional help.

Luckily, for the Ox, although he was inadvertently embroiled in a violent crime of pas-

The terrified boy scrambled to safety through the room's breakfast chute...

...he has become an outspoken advocate on problem gambling...

sion when just a boy, he is now able to live a more effective life.

Freed from the demons that plagued him, he has become an outspoken advocate on problem gambling, creating some good out of the evil of his father's slaying, and is a successful media sports commentator.

IF AT FIRST YOU DONT SUCCEED...

Andrew Kalajzich

The killer was tall, in his mid-40s and of foreign appearance.

Andrew Kalajzich volunteered this information to police after they found the body of his wife, Megan, on the couples' bedroom floor in their Manly house.

Megan had received two fatal gunshot wounds to the face and police retrieved two bullets from her husband's pillow. Initial investigations revealed that, strangely, forced entry into the couple's bedroom had not occurred, so they assumed the murderer had accessed the building from the upstairs balcony.

This homicide was not the first attempt on Megan Kalajzich's life.

A man wearing a balaclava had reportedly assaulted her just two weeks prior to her January 1986 death. There had also been four attempts made on her life in the proceeding weeks leading to her eventual murder. The hapless woman also narrowly escaped death 13 years earlier when both she and her son, Andrew Kalajzich Junior, emerged unscathed from a car crash after Andrew Kalajzich Senior reportedly blacked out while driving the vehicle. Miraculously, the husband recovered from the blackout quickly enough to allow himself

This homicide was not the first attempt on Megan Kalajzich's life.

... he employed an attractive young woman and the pair began a volatile extra-marital affair.

and his family to jump to safety before the out-of-control car crashed into an embankment.

Andrew Kalajzich Senior originally emigrated from Yugoslavia to Sydney. His food, retail and property development interests flourished, and he became a wealthy man. In one of his fish and chip shops, he employed an attractive young woman, Lydia Iurman, and the pair began a volatile extra-marital affair.

Initially, Iurman anticipated the relationship would culminate in marriage, but Kalajzich constantly recanted this commitment at short notice. During these turbulent times, it was also rumoured that Kalajzich was courting his secretary, Marlene Watson. More spice was added to the confusion of real or imagined affairs when Kalajzich reportedly urged his security officer, Warren Elkins, to locate a hit man to terminate the life of his wife Megan.

'Black George' Canellis was the first hired gun to be recruited, offered $25 000 for the contract killing. Canellis reneged on the arrangement after seeing his intended victim for the first time, but still allegedly pocketed $5 000.

It would be Bill Vandenberg who would eventually successfully pull the murder off.

However, problems threatened to derail what was becoming an almost farcical situation. On five occasions, a locked door at the rear of the building caused the homicide to be aborted. Finally, Vandenberg shot Megan Kalajzich and Andrew Kalajzich then escorted the killer from the building, locking the door from inside.

Following the murder, Elkins became a suspect while Canellis, anxious to demonstrate his innocence, agreed to wire himself for potentially incriminating conversations with the alleged killer. Vandenberg admitted his guilt after police raided his flat, with them then taking Vandenbreg, Henry Orrock, Elkins and Kalajzich Senior into custody on 15 February 1986.

During investigation procedures, Marlene Watson firmly denied she had any sexual or romantic involvement with Andrew Kalajzich, while Iurman claimed her relationship had long ago ended after she tired of being repeatedly stood up. Eventually, charges against the wealthy tycoon were dropped due to the lack of a clear motive.

The drama worthy of a soap opera was, however, far from over.

Although cleared, Kalajzich attempted to bribe Vandenberg into making the false claim that he was not involved in the homicide. This reckless move backfired when a frightened Vandenberg strongly implicated Kalajzich,

On five occasions, a locked door at the rear of the building caused the homicide to be aborted.

who was consequently rearrested.

In 1988, at the conclusion of court proceedings, the Judge handed down the verdict—Vandenberg, Orrock and Andrew Kalajzich Senior received life imprisonment, while Elkins received a ten-year term for conspiring to murder Megan Kalajzich. Vandenberg blamed himself for the harsh sentence Orrock received, and the remorseful murderer later hung himself in his prison cell.

...the remorseful murderer later hung himself in his prison cell.

Andrew Kalajzich had an appeal against his sentence rejected, but the obsessive man continued to spend his vast wealth on gaining freedom. Finally his money ran out, but not before he reportedly outlaid up to $100 000 a week on legal fees. During his long and turbulent time in custody, Kalajzich survived a 1993 knife attack in Lithgow Prison.

Marlene Watson, his mother, his mother-in-law and the famous radio host Alan Jones were amongst Kalajzich's regular visitors, all of who supported his claims of innocence.

Regardless, yet another appeal was rejected in 1998 and he remains in prison, guilty as charged. He will be eligible for parole in late 2011.

THE PUPPET MASTER

On 24 February 1988, the house Christine Hicks owned and shared with horse trainer and habitual criminal, Allen Hall, burnt to the ground, just after the couple had begun a serious de facto relationship.

Cec Waters

Following the destruction of the house, they received a sinister warning in the form of a handwritten note stating 'more is to come'. The lovers were convinced that the culprit was Cec Waters, well-known boxing trainer and Christine's former partner.

Cec was father and trainer to three formidable professional boxers—Guy and Troy Waters, both Commonwealth champions, and Dean Waters, the Australian heavyweight titleholder.

One night, four months after the destruction of Christine's house, barking dogs woke Hall from his slumber. In the nearby bushes, Dean Waters and his gym trainer Damon Cooper watched Hall searching in the darkness for intruders, before shooting and fatally wounding him.

Police later placed Dean Waters near the murder scene when they found a footprint matching the tread of his runners. They charged both Cooper and him with Halls' murder and Cec Waters as an accessory.

...they received a sinister warning in the form of a handwritten note stating 'more is to come'.

...the vengeful father had long dominated every word and action of his sons...

It soon became apparent that the vengeful father had long dominated every word and action of his sons and Cooper, like some evil puppet master, and was behind the homicide of the man who had replaced him in Christine Hicks' affections.

Twenty years younger than Hicks, after terminating their abusive de facto relationship, Hicks had taken out an Aggravated Violence Order (AVO) against Cec and become Allen Hall's live-in lover. Waters, bitter at being so spurned and replaced, convinced son Dean and Cooper that Christine Hicks had to die. Ominously, by May 1988, two fresh graves had been dug in nearby Ourimbah State Forest. It was 29 June 1988 when Dean Waters and Cooper acted on the puppet master's demands, using a 12-gauge shotgun and a .22 rifle to kill Allen Hall. Cec Waters, however, remained unimpressed, as the killers spared the life of the woman who had become a surrogate mother to his sons.

In their July 1989 court case, the defendants received unexpected reprieves when the magistrate dismissed all charges against them due to insufficient evidence.

However, on 8 February 1997, nearly a decade after the Hall homicide, a dramatic new development occurred. Dean Waters presented himself at the nearby Wyong Police Station, confessing to the 1988 killing of Hall.

Dean Waters and Damon Cooper faced fresh murder charges, with police once more naming Cec Waters as an accessory. The latter denied all charges, but died of a heart attack before his trial began.

In court, Dean Waters pleaded not guilty to murder on the grounds of diminished responsibility, before indicating he was prepared to plead guilty to manslaughter. Psychiatric reports presented in court greatly influenced the final verdicts. The defence alleged Cec Waters had subjected his sons to harsh beatings for many years and had previously openly encouraged a sexual relationship between Hall and Hicks. His brutal domination of Dean Waters, in particular, provided compelling evidence.

On 31 July 1997, the court cleared Dean Waters of all charges.

Damon Cooper was not so fortunate.

Sentenced to a custodial sentence of 18 years with a non-parole period of 12 years, Cooper went on to appeal unsuccessfully against the severity of his sentence.

Dean Waters and Damon Cooper faced fresh murder charges...

CHAPTER 2

CRIMES OF THE TIMES (1990s-PRESENT)

LONG WAIT FOR JUSTICE

A homicide mystery that tantalised Sydney residents for 13 years finally came to a fitting conclusion on 21 November 2008 when a jury found 46-year-old Gordon Wood guilty of murdering his girlfriend, Caroline Byrne, just 24-years-old at the time of her death.

At first, it was widely believed the glamorous model had committed suicide after her body was found in June 1995 at the bottom of a high cliff near the mouth of Sydney harbour.

This area of the city, commonly known as 'the Gap', had a notorious reputation as a suicide location and Byrne herself had suffered depression at times, notably in the years following her mother's suicide in 1992.

Three years previously, friends of the dead woman believed she was planning to end her relationship with Wood, who had become overly possessive of her. By then,

Caroline Byrne

...he was allegedly ringing Byrne ten times a day and possibly stalking her.

he was allegedly ringing Byrne ten times a day and possibly stalking her.

Her supporters also maintained Wood had decided to silence Byrne, permanently, to prevent her revealing potentially damaging information about his business activities. In 1995, he was chauffeur to Rene Rivkin, the flamboyant stockbroker who would go on to commit suicide a decade later after serving a prison sentence for insider trading. Both Rivkin and Wood had previously been shareholders in Sydney's Offset Alpine Printing Company, which burnt down in mysterious circumstances on Christmas Eve, 1993.

After Byrne's death, Wood consistently denied he had killed Ms Byrne.

He claimed he was ferrying Rivkin and former Labor senator Graham Richardson to and from an Italian restaurant on the day she died. Then, when she failed to return to their home, he notified police and was 'guided by her spirit' to lead detectives to his girlfriend's car near the Gap. From that point on, Byrne's family members became suspicious of Wood and his possible involvement in her death.

In 1998 after the second 'open' finding in the inquest, Wood left Australia, for some years residing in various parts of Europe and London, where he worked as a business consultant and gym instructor.

However, the case was far from over.

A task force, 'Strikeforce Irondale', was established in 2000. Hundreds of witnesses were interviewed, during which time Caroline's father Tony Byrne waged an ongoing campaign to see Wood brought to justice.

In 2004, scientific reports relating to the physics of a body falling from the cliff intimated it was more likely that Caroline Byrne had been thrown from it 'like a spear' due to the position of the body being at least three metres from the edge of the Gap. This encouraged the Crown to push for a trial of Gordon Wood and, in April 2006, he was extradited to Sydney where later in June at Wood's committal hearing a damaging revelation surfaced.

A letter allegedly written by him to his friend, Brett Cochrane on 16 May 1996, was produced in which Wood referred to 'covering up for the boss' and 'having to do his dirty work'. He also complained that Rene Rivkin was avoiding him, and reneging on a previous agreement to help Wood finance a share trading company.

'I'm glad it's over', stated the author, 'except I still haven't seen the money promised to me from the Offset Alpine deal…'

After court proceedings began in early August 2008, the prosecution suffered a setback—the trial was aborted due to jury

Gordon Wood

…the physics of a body falling from the cliff intimated it was more likely that Byrne had been thrown…

...Byrne's murder was not premeditated, but rather a 'sudden, homicidal rage'...

misconduct. However, once the trial resumed, the jury was convinced by the prosecution's case, which claimed Caroline Byrne's murder was not premeditated, but rather a 'sudden, homicidal rage' brought on by Wood's perceived need to protect his employment and financial security.

On 21 November 2008, Gordon Wood was found guilty of murdering Caroline Byrne, and on 4 December, he was sentenced to 17 years imprisonment.

Wood still stridently maintains his 'not guilty' plea, claiming the reason he has shown no contrition or remorse for Byrne's death is due to his supposed innocence. This unwillingness to admit guilt might indicate that it is likely the Byrne family's quest for justice will be tested once more sometime in the future when Wood's defence appeals the case once more.

PARADISE LOST

'It has the charm of yesterday, without the burden of tomorrow.'

This is how Australian author, Tim Latham, described the tranquil paradise of Norfolk Island, with its pleasant climate, the fertility of its volcanic soil, and the absence of flies, mosquitoes and snakes, all of which make it very conducive for human occupation.

The tiny eight-by-five kilometre island was an English penal colony between 1774 and 1855, after which it was abandoned until 1856 when Pitcairn islanders, the descendants of Tahitians and the famous Bounty mutineers, were re-located there.

Today, the local population of nearly 2,000 elects its own government and proudly fly their own distinctive national flag, on which is displayed the famous Norfolk Pine. The renowned novelist, Colleen McCulloch (*The Thorn Birds*) is a resident, and the population are generally considered very laidback and friendly.

However, sometime around midday 31 March 2002, on a balmy Easter Sunday, Norfolk Island lost its innocence when 29-year-old Janelle Patton was herself virtually crucified. Her body was found, covered with black plastic sheeting, at a reserve on a well-used island

Janelle Patton

Her body was found, covered with black plastic sheeting, at a reserve on a well-used island...

The murdered woman had suffered 64 stab wounds, a broken pelvis, broken ribs and a fractured skull...

road. The murdered woman had suffered 64 stab wounds, a broken pelvis, broken ribs and a fractured skull, in what appeared to have been a frenzied attack. Those who later viewed the crime scene at the public reserve were traumatised by the experience. Janelle Patton's death had not been an accident or peaceful in any way—someone had literally butchered her.

No witnesses came forward to volunteer information to Australian Federal Police investigators about the brutal slaying and, as the months slipped by, the secretive and perhaps protective community produced no definite suspects. Rumours about the former convict settlement's first murder in 150 years could not be stifled, but, despite many suspected motives, no murder weapon was found and the limited forensic evidence available contained no items for DNA analysis.

Hopes increased after blurred palm prints were discovered on the black plastic, but less than half of the 2,700 people who were on the island on that fateful day accepted the voluntary invitation to provide finger prints to the frustrated investigation team.

Over two years elapsed, during which time the reward offered for information about the killing rose from $50 000 to over $300 000. While nothing may have emerged to help police find the killer, some personal information surfaced about Patten herself. The attractive, argumentative and hard drinking victim had allegedly been involved in many sexual relationships with both married and single men during the two years she had worked as a domestic worker on Norfolk Island.

Glenn McNeill

Consequently, there was no shortage of suspects among many local men and women adversely affected by Janelle Patton's promiscuous behaviour, and some 16 'persons of interest' (including Patten's parents) were named.

Regardless, in June 2004, Coroner Ron Cahill delivered an open finding at an inquest into the murder.

Six months later, in December, new developments in the perplexing case arose.

Just prior to Christmas, police confiscated an unregistered 1984 white Honda sedan, which they painstakingly examined. The focus of the investigation dramatically shifted to a chef living in Nelson, on New Zealand's South Island—28-year-old, Glenn McNeill.

In February 2005, police arrested him, declaring they had made a DNA breakthrough and after two hours of questioning he admitted guilt. The father of two claimed he had accidentally run over Ms Patton following a heavy session of cannabis smoking. He then allegedly stabbed the young woman 'a few times' in an apparent attempt to avoid detection.

...he had accidentally run over Ms Patton following a heavy session of cannabis smoking.

...the 29-year-old dismissed the original confession made to police as 'complete rubbish'...

The court case was conducted in the historic Norfolk Island courthouse in February 2007, almost five years after the murder, with McNeill entering a plea of 'not guilty'. In an unsworn statement, the 29-year-old dismissed the original confession made to police as 'complete rubbish', telling the jury he had mental health problems at the time.

'I did not murder Janelle Patton,' he told the court.

The month-long trial ended on 8 March.

After an 11-hour deliberation, the jury found McNeill guilty of murdering Janelle Patton. The defence team indicated an appeal against the verdict was possible, but it was obvious that most members of the relieved island community warmly received the decision.

On 25 July, the Norfolk Island Supreme Court sentenced McNeill to 24 years in custody with a non-parole period of 18 years, which he is currently serving in a NSW prison due to there being no facilities for long-term prisoners on the island.

An appeal against his sentence was dismissed in May 2008.

DIVER STILL IN DEEP WATER

*A grave injustice and
an embarrassment to Australia'.*

('Tina' Watson's family)

*'It ('Gabe' Watson's sentence) should
have been six years."*

(A US investigator)

*'The handling of this sad case
has been absolutely deplorable.'*

(Lawrence Springborg, then leader
of the Queensland Opposition parties)

'We couldn't prove it.'

(Queensland Director of
Public Prosecution, Tony Moynihan)

These were some of the responses after 32-year-old David Gabriel 'Gabe' Watson successfully entered a plea bargain defence to the charge of murdering his 26-year-old former wife, Christine 'Tina' Watson.

The defendant was expected to receive a minimum custodial sentence of four years and six months for a manslaughter conviction. When he was only jailed for 12 months, the deceased woman's family, American law-enforcement authorities and politicians were outraged at the perceived leniency of the

**Watson
successfully
entered a
plea bargain
defence to
the charge of
murdering his
former wife...**

Christine Watson was a petite bride of just 11 days when she drowned on the Great Barrier Reef...

sentence for the Alabama resident.

Christine Watson was a petite bride of just 11 days when she drowned on the Great Barrier Reef off Townsville on 22 October 2003. On her Australian honeymoon, the American woman was scuba diving near the 'Yongala' shipwreck with her husband Gabe, an experienced diver.

The powerfully built bubble-wrap salesman later claimed,

'We were together. Then I went up, and she went all the way down.'

At the 2007 inquest (which Watson refused to leave America to attend), a diving photographer submitted that, on the day of the fatality, Watson returned alone to the tour boat, shouting for help. After Tina's body was recovered, Cardiac Pulmonary Resuscitation (CPR) was applied, but she failed to respond.

Suspicions about Watson's true role in his wife's death heated upon his return to Alabama, where authorities discovered him to be the beneficiary of a US$160 000 life insurance policy his wife had finalised before she embarked on her honeymoon trip. Investigators also believed Watson might have been jealous about a brief alleged affair Tina had with another man prior to her marriage.

When local Federal Bureau of Investigation officers (FBI) and Queensland detectives raided his house in Alabama, Watson was declared a murder suspect. They seized documents, photographs and a computer containing details about the Barrier Reef diving trip, and Watson was interviewed on at least 25 occasions.

In November 2007, at a Townsville inquest into Christine Watson's death, over 60 witnesses provided direct or phoned evidence. When the hearings concluded, it was recommended Gabe Watson be charged with murder.

The case came before the courts in 2009, at which time the prosecution claimed Watson had deliberately switched off his wife's air supply when they were scuba diving six years previously. However, the court accepted the defendant's assertion that he panicked when Tina became distressed, causing him to accidentally kill her, and brought down the 12 month sentence.

...deliberately switched off his wife's air supply when they were scuba diving...

US investigators claimed they were not informed about Gabe Watson's plea-bargain negotiations with Queensland authorities and that there was a strong possibility Watson could be charged with murder in the United States when he was extradited back to his home country after completing his sentence in Australia.

On 18 June 2009, Cameron Dick, Queensland's Attorney-General, announced the state government would appeal against the leniency of Gabe Watson's sentence and, in September, much to the outcry of those who believed him culpable of murder, his sentence was increased by a mere 6 months.

Despite avoiding the full weight of the law, when Watson is released from jail in 2010, Alabama Attorney General Troy King has made it clear he will go after him for capital murder, the worst category of murder in the state.

Watson faces death by lethal injection or life without parole...

If convicted, Watson faces death by lethal injection or life without parole, yet he could escape extradition back to the US on one key ground: the Commonwealth will not allow people to be extradited for crimes punishable by the death penalty.

In a strange twist to the crime, in mid-November 2009, Tina Watson's father revealed to the press he believed his daughter might have been the victim of a copycat murder. Nearly a decade earlier, despite being an experienced diver (unlike Tina Watson), Shelley Tyre lost her life in a diving accident in the Caribbean. Her husband, David Swain, was recently convicted for her murder after getting away with what appeared to be the perfect crime.

Watson's father believes that the parallels between the crimes are so close that it is highly credible Tyre's murder acted as a blueprint for his daughter's murder. He also argues that the successful prosecution of Swain spoke volumes to the lack of justice for his daughter and has continued to fight for Gabe Watson to be held accountable for his crimes.

Christine and David Watson

A FATAL INFATUATION

Joe Korp

On the surface, Joe and Maria Korp may have appeared a typical suburban couple, but all was not well in their world in the Melbourne suburb of Mickleham.

Maria had revealed to a close friend that she feared for her marriage—no surprises, given their unconventional life-style, which involved membership of a swingers' dating club. Unbeknownst to Maria, 47-year-old Joe was engaged in an ongoing affair with 38-year-old Tania Herman, who he had met through the club's internet service.

Things reached breaking point in December 2004.

Maria obtained an intervention order against her husband, who was ordered not to attend or damage the Mickleham property they co-owned.

Several months later, on Tuesday 8 February 2005, Maria attended Broadmeadows Magistrates Court, asking police to drop the intervention order. Joe was with her, and court officials noted at the time that she appeared somewhat nervous and agitated.

The following day, Joe reported his wife missing when she failed to collect their son after school.

Four days passed until Maria resurfaced,

...reported his wife missing when she failed to collect their son after school.

albeit in the most distressing of ways. She was found unconscious in the locked boot of her maroon Mazda, not far from one of Melbourne's famous landmarks, the Shrine of Remembrance, and immediately admitted to intensive care, her condition critical. Presenting to the media, her distraught husband said the past days had been 'like having a nightmare but you don't wake up…your stomach just keeps turning.'

Maria Korp

She was found unconscious in the locked boot of her maroon Mazda…

While the 50-year-old Maria remained in a coma, police questioned both Korp and Herman. Korp maintained he loved his wife, strongly proclaiming his innocence. However, Tania Herman disputed this, claiming her lover had persuaded her to strangle Maria so that the couple would be free to establish a permanent relationship.

Herman alleged Joe Korp carefully packed a bag containing 'bizarre' items for his smitten lover to use in the planned assault. In the early hours of that fateful February morning, Korp met Herman at her flat and drove her back to his own palatial home where she hid in the dark garage. Before returning to have breakfast with his wife, who would leave for work as early as 6.30am, he supposedly uttered the following advice to his lover,

'You've got to do it for us. Don't let the bitch come out of here alive.'

Entering the garage, Herman, wearing a swimming cap, balaclava, pair of Joe's over-size boots and cotton gloves, brutally attacked Maria. The besieged woman cried out three times to her daughter, Laura, for help, something Laura would later recall hearing but assumed at the time was the muffled crying of a child in a nearby house.

Being younger and a tri-athlete, and thus much stronger than her unsuspecting victim, Herman was too formidable to defend against. In a vicious and swift attack, she choked Maria with the leather strap of a handbag until she was unconscious. Herman then dumped Maria in the boot of the Mazda and drove her into the city, but fled after panicking when, believing Maria to be dead, she heard her victim moving around in the boot.

... she choked Maria with the leather strap of a handbag until she was unconscious.

On 16 February, Joe Korp and Tania Herman were charged with attempted murder, conspiracy to commit murder and intention to cause serious bodily harm.

Herman offered testimony against Korp in an attempt to gain a reduced sentence, receiving 12 years in custody with a minimum non-parole period of nine years. The infatu-ated woman, who obviously once believed Joe Korp to be her soul mate, appeared remorse-ful about her actions. Presiding Judge Bernard Teague described her future chances of rehabilitation as being excellent.

Korp pleaded not guilty to all charges.

Regardless, he was ordered to stand trial on 4 August 2005, before being released on bail. When, upon the order of the public advocate, doctors removed life support care to Maria the following day, the more serious charge of murder arose as she died without regaining consciousness.

A week later, a large crowd attended Maria's funeral, with much media attention focussing on her children.

Joe Korp was noticeably absent.

That night, he was found hanging in a shed behind their home with the presumption he had committed suicide. Near the body was an emotional video diary, whose contents proclaimed Joe Korp's innocence and his never-ending love for his wife.

This, however, was not to be the conclusion of the sordid story.

At an inquest in 2006, it was alleged that the planning of Maria Korp's death was detailed and meticulous. In the months leading up to Maria's final attempted murder, both Joe Korp and Tania Herman had discussions with other parties about the ways and means of disposing of Maria, with Joe even indicating he was prepared to pay up to $20 000 to see the job done.

Near the body was an emotional video diary, whose contents proclaimed Joe Korp's innocence...

Of course, all this comes from the mouth of Tania Herman, the only surviving witness and perpetrator of the attempted murder, who it might be argued would have some interest in passing all of the blame and intention onto the shoulder of Joe Korp.

Thus, we may never know the truth, the whole truth and nothing but the truth.

Maybe it's better we don't.

A CHILD ABANDONED

A short section of security video, taken at Southern Cross Railway Station in Melbourne on 15 September 2007, would shock the nation, yet capture its heart.

In the grainy footage, a small girl, dressed in a cheerful red jumper, seems obediently to adhere to her father's instructions to wait at the foot of an escalator. Little does the poor child know, he will never return.

As he strides away, suitcase in hand, he is bound for the airport, destination USA.

The small girl, dubbed 'Pumpkin' by authorities (after the brand of clothing she was wearing at the time), and the short segment of security footage would be the keys to solving a crime of passion that had occurred just days before in New Zealand.

An An Liu, a Chinese National, had moved from China to New Zealand to learn English in 2002. She moved into the residence of Nai Yin Xue, a martial arts instructor, as a tenant, cleaning for her board. Eventually, to avoid her deportation, the pair married.

Reports are, initially, despite an age difference of over 20 years, the relationship was without too much trouble. However, after the birth of their daughter, Qian, the couple experienced difficulties. Nai Yin was becoming

Eventually, to avoid her deportation, the pair married.

increasingly jealous, seeing any small thing, even as much as a friendly 'hello kiss' offered to An An, as a threat to their relationship.

...held a knife to his wife's stomach, threatening to stab her if she was in any way disloyal to him.

This finally boiled over when Xue held a knife to his wife's stomach, threatening to stab her if she was in any way disloyal to him. An An fled with her small daughter to China, but returned when her husband pleaded that he wanted to make their relationship work. This was despite being charged for assault over the incident.

Unfortunately, upon her return, nothing had really changed, and so she left him once more, moving to Wellington. A witness would later allege she saw an axe in Xue's car around this time, which he told her he had taken to Wellington when he had gone in search of his wife. Searching the boarding house where she was staying, he had found her door locked, saying later 'his wife was lucky he hadn't found her.'

This, however, was just the prelude to An An Xue's eventual demise.

On 11 September 2007, Nai Yin Xue finally did track down his wayward wife and with a simple necktie, ended her life. After strangling her, he loaded her into the boot of the car and returned home to their Mt Roskill home in Auckland. He left the car parked at the front of the property, the body in all likelihood still in the boot, fleeing to Australia two days later.

After the famous dumping of his defenceless child at Southern Cross, he fled yet again, this time to Los Angeles, California, where he went into hiding. With the discovery of Pumpkin in Melbourne, the search began for her missing mother, whose semi-naked body was found on 19 September in the boot of the car dumped by Nai Yin a week before.

Despite the police listing An An's death as 'violent', they did not initially lay any public blame on her fugitive husband, instead appealing to him to come forward to help them with their investigations. This appeal was quickly set aside and a warrant for Nai Yin's arrest was issued, with US officials asked to help track down the suspected murderer.

Months passed, with few leads until mid-February 2008 when witnesses reported having seen a man matching the suspect's appearance in Texas. On 29 February, in the Atlanta, Georgia, suburb of Chamblee, police received a call from a group of local Chinese residents who believed they had the man wanted for questioning.

Police jumped at the tip-off, arriving at the caller's residence to find the do-gooders had made a citizen's arrest— Nai Yin was found by law enforcement officers with his pants around

After the famous dumping of his defenceless child at Southern Cross, he fled yet again...

his ankles and his hands tied with his own belt. He was taken into custody and almost immediately deported to New Zealand, where he was held on remand until his hearing on 4 September.

Pleading not guilty, Nai Yin was sentenced to stand trial in June 2009.

This trial, however, would not be as cut and dry as prosecutors had hoped it would.

Although the evidence seemed overwhelmingly against Xue, his defence team deftly painted a very different picture. His lawyer, Chris Comeskey, alluded to the court that An An was in fact straying from the relationship. She had allegedly told a friend on the chat network QQ that she had been with a young man who made her feel as 'sexually ferocious as a wolf'.

Three lots of DNA found in the dead woman's underwear (that of Xue and two other unidentified persons) seemed to back up this theory. Comeskey eventually proposed to the court that An An had in fact died by sexual misadventure (erotic asphyxiation) at the hands of one of the unknown others who, according to the DNA samples, seemed to have sexual access to her. It was under the belief that his wife was cheating on him that Xue left her, heartbroken, taking their daughter as punishment, with no idea that she had

...that An An had in fact died by sexual misadventure...

in fact been killed.

The Crown Prosecutor labelled such claims as preposterous, countering in his closing summation that there was an 'avalanche of evidence' to convict Xue. The jury agreed with, finding him guilty as charged. As the verdict was read out, Xue protested loudly, pumping his fist in the air, yelling 'unfair, unfair'. He continued to contest the verdict as police took him to his cell, proclaiming his innocence.

On 31 July, Xue remained quiet and stony-faced as he received a minimum non-parole period of 12 years for the crime. In his sentencing, Justice Williams made it clear that, given evidence of previous violence in the relationship and the actions following the murder, in particular the abandonment of his daughter Xue, deserved more than the minimum non-parole period.

Comeskey addressed the media after the decision, telling them that Xue 'maintains in no way is he responsible for the death,' and that an appeal was a given. In September 2009, he laid the grounds for appeal, including the fact that the jury were not sequestered during the deliberations, meaning they could have been unduly influenced in their decision. Other reasons included the fairness of the trial and the effect of the judge's summing up.

As yet, no court date for the appeal has

As the verdict was read out, Xue protested loudly, pumping his fist in the air, yelling 'unfair, unfair'.

...Xue remains behind bars at Rimutaka Prison in Upper Hut, New Zealand...

been set, and Xue remains behind bars at Rimutaka Prison in Upper Hut, New Zealand, where he is apparently looking forward to the appeal.

And little 'Pumpkin'?

She now lives with her grandmother in China, who was given custody of her following the torrid incident, and is reportedly well and happy despite the tragedy which unfolded around her.

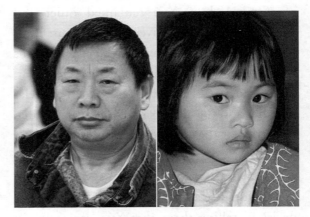

Nai Yin Xue and 'Pumpkin'

REPEAT OFFENDER

'I'm not working for you anymore.'

This was the succinct phone message Leigh Robinson delivered to his boss mid-morning on 28 April 2008.

There were compelling reasons for his sudden resignation—an hour before, the 60-year-old truck driver had remorselessly shot dead his recent former lover, Tracey Greenbury.

This was not the first time Robinson had committed a crime of passion. Forty years earlier, the enraged 20-year-old had murdered another former girlfriend, 17-year-old Valerie Ethel Dunn, in her Chadstone home. Robinson believed Dunn had been unfaithful, stabbing her 16 times with a carving knife in a vicious attack of jealousy and revenge.

'I'm just sorry these things happen, but I don't know why they did,' stated the apparently remorseful killer after his savage slaying of Dunn.

Unimpressed, the presiding judge at his trial sentenced Robinson to death after his guilty verdict. The Victorian Governor at the time, Sir Rohan Delacombe, on the advice of Cabinet reduced the sentence to life imprisonment, and Robinson's subsequent good behaviour in custody led to his release after serving

Leigh Robinson

Robinson believed Dunn had been unfaithful, stabbing her 16 times with a carving knife...

only 15 years.

Initially, Robinson appeared to be a reformed man, but by the 1990's was back in custody after being found guilty of rape and for possessing stolen goods valued at $100 000. When he met Tracey Greenbury, a 33-year-old mother of two with a history of drug dependency, Robinson admitted to her he had served custodial sentences in the past.

She believed him a reformed man, but upon discovering that he had a 1990s conviction for rape, Greenbury confronted her lover outside the caravan where he lived on his boss's Pearcedale property, informing him she was going to end their relationship.

His violent reaction was terrifying in the extreme.

Leigh Robinson grabbed the young woman's hair and dragged her into his caravan where he held her at gunpoint for a couple of hours.

'Don't push my buttons. You're pushing me too far', he apparently warned the petrified Greenbury.

Max Greenbury, father of the victim, was placated when Robinson reassured him in a phone conversation, laughing and joking, that he would never actually harm Tracey. Unfortunately for the woman, both father and daughter took him at his word, ignoring the fact that

...dragged her into his caravan where he held her at gunpoint for a couple of hours.

Robinson had openly gloated about Tracey's obvious fear as he held a .12 gauge shot gun to her head.

A week later, Robinson brutally disposed of Tracey Greenbury with a shot to the back of the head as she huddled in the doorway of the house of her neighbour, Leoni Coates.

Police mounted a massive two-day manhunt and, in the early hours of 30 April 2008, a heavily armed officer from the Special Operations Group apprehended Leigh Robinson near the Princes Highway in the outer Melbourne suburb of Eumemmerring.

Charged with murder, Robinson claimed he shot Greenbury accidentally when he went to rescue her as she fell, a defence described by prosecutor Peter Rose SC as 'so fanciful it beggars belief'.

On 29 September 2009, much to the relief of Greenbury's family, Robinson was found guilty of Tracey's murder, with Justice Simon Whelan remanding him in custody for sentencing at a later date. The Crown indicated at the time it would be seeking life imprisonment, without parole.

Unfortunately, for the Greenbury family, this relief was short-lived.

At a pre-sentencing hearing on 17 December 2009, Robinson's lawyer informed the court he would be appealing the murder con-

Robinson claimed he shot Greenbury accidentally...

viction in the Court of Appeal. This should occur sometime in 2010 and until then the Greenbury's hope for an end to this terrible affair will be held at bay.

A LOVE THAT COULD ONLY END IN DEATH

'If I can't have her, no one can.'

So read part of the chilling suicide note of 37-year-old Lechmana Nanthagopal.

It went on to say,

'As you know, I love Pharzana very much and every time she says she wants to leave me it breaks my heart to pieces—hurts me to pieces... When you find this letter I will probably be dead too.'

Despite arming himself with a bottle of sleeping pills and two bottles of bourbon, Lechmana would never get to fulfil his wish to end his own life. Acting on a tip-off, in the early morning of 25 February 2008, just hours after the man had killed his wife of six years, police managed to arrest him near The Gap in Watson's Bay.

The bloodied body of his wife, 27-year-old Pharzana Nanthagopal, was found in the couple's North Parramatta apartment by her parents who lived nearby after Lechmana called to tell them she was dead.

In another room, thankfully, was their unharmed four-year-old daughter.

Having lived half of their married life with Ms Nanthagopal's parents, it was apparent that the relationship was in troubled waters, with

...arming himself with a bottle of sleeping pills and two bottles of bourbon...

them witnessing many arguments between their daughter and her husband. The couple had been seeing a marriage counsellor and both were diagnosed as clinically depressed.

In the months leading up to their daughter's death, the arguments grew worse, to the point where it was clear to them that the relationship was unhappy and becoming untenable.

Unable to stand it any longer, Pharzana demanded a trial separation in November 2007. Lechmana, desperate to keep the relationship, even went to the lengths of asking Pharzana's mother to try to persuade her to change her mind.

...he took matters into his own hands —literally— strangling his wife.

Then, something in Lechmana snapped, and sometime between 3.00 and 3.30am on 25 February, he took matters into his own hands—literally—strangling his wife. Not long after he left for 'The Gap', presumably, as his note implied, to end his own life.

Shortly after 3.30am, Pharzana's mother answered the phone, only to hear an eerie 'gurgling' noise on the end of the line. She would later describe it as though the person was drowning and trying to get their breath. A short while later, Lechmana called to say in a calm, cold voice that their daughter was dead.

After hospitalisation for minor injuries sustained during his capture, Lechmana was remanded without bail to appear before the court again in April for a committal hearing, later being sent for trial on the charge of murder.

Using his depression as evidence of not being of sound mind, Lechmana's defence argued that the charge of murder should be dropped for the lesser charge of manslaughter. Whether Justice Megan Latham accepts this remains to be seen as the case was still before the courts at the time of print.

AUSTRALIA'S OWN LORENA BOBBITT?

Rajini Narayan

On 7 December 2008, the fire brigade pulled up at a blazing house fire in the Adelaide suburb of Unley and, despite their best efforts, witnessed the suburban home end up gutted.

This was no ordinary fire.

Police soon discovered that one of the occupants of the dwelling, 44-year-old Rajini Narayan, had started the fire under the most unusual of circumstances—by setting fire to the penis of her husband, 47-year-old Satish Narayan. In what could be construed as the basest crime of passion, Rajini's jealousy possessed her. Fearing Satish was having an affair, she decided to ensure her man was hers and hers alone.

It is alleged that on that summer's eve, she doused her husband's penis in methylated spirits as he slept, then set fire to him. In all probability, waking in fright and pain, Satish Narayan then knocked over the bottle of 'metho' as he rose from the bed, sparking the major blaze.

Suffering from major burns, he died several weeks later.

At her initial hearing in January 2009, the court heard that Ms Narayan had told neighbours,

...she doused her husband's penis in methylated spirits as he slept...

'I'm a jealous wife, his penis should belong to me, I just wanted to burn his penis so it belongs to me and no one else...I didn't mean this to happen.'

The case against Ms Narayan was adjourned until 30 October. She was released into home detention, despite a psychologist's report indicating that she did not fully understand how her actions could be construed as premeditation, and thus that the charge of murder could be laid.

She was released into home detention...

When she appeared before the courts again in October, her case was further adjourned until December, with her defence counsel, Lindy Powell QC, believing her client was still not yet prepared properly to answer to the charge of murder.

What it will take to help Ms Narayan realise her actions caused the death of her husband, and how she will answer to this, remains to be seen. When she finally faces a judge and jury, the court case will no doubt be one of major public interest.

BLACKTOWN MURDERS

Jyoti Mehta

A seemingly innocent family drive one autumn night to the Blue Mountains was far from innocent.

Unbeknown to the car's occupants, bar the driver, in the boot were the slain bodies of a young child and woman—38-year-old Jyoti Mehta and nine-year-old Ujalla Dinesh, the wife and stepdaughter of 41-year-old Sanjay Mehta.

Sanjay, employed as a parking technician, had met Jyoti on the internet in July 2006. She then moved to Australia in May the following year to marry him. Both had live-in children from a previous marriage.

Unfortunately, for Jyoti, the relationship quickly turned sour.

Not long after she arrived in Australia, the arguments began. Sanjay took her passport so that she could not flee home, checked calls made on her phone and restricted access to the computer. Neighbours would see Ujalla happily playing outside the house in the outer north-western suburb of Blacktown, but this was underscored by the sound of arguments often emanating from inside the dwelling.

In January 2009, Jyoti contacted the Jessie Street Domestic Violence Service after being verbally abused by her husband—he

...in the boot were the slain bodies of a young child and woman...

had threatened to kill her or have her deported. Poonam Sharma, Jyoti's sister, also became progressively concerned about the nature of the relationship after being informed by Jyoti that Sanjay was resisting any attempts at helping her get her permanent residency.

With the relationship clearly on the rocks, a troubled Sanjay could see himself losing control of his fiancée. Fearing she would leave him, he took action. In their home, sometime in the first week of May, he murdered her, also taking the life of her daughter, who it is believed probably witnessed the crime.

Needing to dispose of the bodies, he slung them into the boot of his car then gathered some family members together on the pretext of taking a casual drive. They headed for the Blue Mountains, eventually arriving at Echo Point. While the family went for a walk, he quickly disposed of the bodies, throwing them over the 150-metre cliff.

...he quickly disposed of the bodies, throwing them over the 150-metre cliff.

Mehta reported the pair missing on 5 May, telling police that both of them, their passports and $100 were gone.

Just on a month later, bushwalkers spotted a body at the base of Echo Point. The long black hair and purple top of the decomposing corpse were a match for the missing Jyoti, and not far from it lay a second smaller corpse—her daughter Ujalla.

Police arrested Mehta on 2 June on suspicion of murder, impounding his car. He strenuously denied the allegations, despite mobile phone records showing he had travelled to the Blue Mountains a month before. With more questioning, he admitted that he had been there, but only in the hope of finding his missing fiancée and step-daughter.

On August 14, the Supreme Court sentenced Mehta to 30 years' imprisonment for the murder of Jyoti and life imprisonment for the murder of Ujalla. Mehta continued to deny involvement right up until the verdict and sentencing, although it is alleged he made a confession to a fellow inmate while on remand.

...it is alleged he made a confession to a fellow inmate while on remand.

In jail now, he has many, many years to meditate on his actions, and the family of Jyoti and Ujalla can rest easy knowing the deaths of their loved ones have been avenged.

A WOMAN TORN ASUNDER

In August 2009, almost 24 years after Vivienne Cameron's abandoned car was found in the waters near the San Remo Bridge, a new mystery was bout to engulf the Victorian island of the 'little penguins' once more.

Around midday on Sunday 16 August, a woman walking her dog along Newhaven beach at Philip Island made a gruesome discovery.

Not far from the bridge, she came across a human leg.

Not far from the bridge, she came across a human leg.

After reporting the shocking find to police, Homicide were immediately on the case, releasing details of a distinguishing mark on the limb they hoped would lead to quick identification of the person to whom the leg belonged.

They believed it was that of a Caucasian female, standing between 172cm and 175cm tall, and the distingushing mark, a tattoo with a distinct floral design, was published in newspapers across the country.

A day later, passengers on the Sorrento to Queenscliff ferry had their peaceful journey shattered when they saw what they believed to be a limb floating in the water. Members of the water police and a Victorian Police helicopter were dispatched to the area but their

Rachael Betts

search proved fruitless.

However, the release of the tattoo did bear fruit—the family of a woman who had not seen her in several days and already reported her missing, came forward in disbelief that the limb might belong to their daughter.

DNA tests followed, confirming their worst nightmares.

The leg was identified as belonging to Rachael Betts of Epping. Rachael, a childcare teacher, had not been seen since 11 August when she told friends she was at the shops in Waterdale Rd in the north-eastern Melbourne suburb of Heidelberg Heights. Putting together a picture of what might have occurred, police believed the casually dressed Betts, carrying a brown clutch bag, had parked her car at Glover St, walked about 500 metres to nearby shops and had met up with a person or persons around 6pm. It was believed she was possibly going on a fishing trip.

In mid-September, reports started filtering through from various sources, hinting at reasons why Rachael had disappeared. A friend came forward saying they believed Betts had fallen in with a 'bad crowd', and that her disappearance might be related to a drug debt.

...her disappearance might be related to a drug debt.

'They fell out. Who knows over what? Someone said it was over a small debt,' a newspaper reported the anonymous friend to have said.

Several others supported this possibility.

Investigations continued, but little came to light until yet another grisly discovery was made in late October. Workers cleaning up a lake in a reserve in the north of Melbourne pulled a black barrel from it, which sat at a factory nearby for several days until a bad smell was noticed emanating from it.

Upon prising it open, human remains were found inside.

Police immediately sent divers into the lake to search for more evidence and DNA tested the contents of the barrel.

Nothing more was found and the testing proved the remains not to be those of Rachael Betts.

Finally, after a painful memorial service for Rachael that occurred with all the attached grief of still not having her body found or any real lead as to the foul play attached to her disappearance, police made a real breakthrough.

On 4 November, after confessing to police the day before, John Leslie Coombs, 55 of Preston, appeared before the Melbourne Magistrate's Court, charged with murder.

The grisly details of Rachael Betts demise finally began to be revealed.

Coombs had often been seen at Betts house by neighbours, who nicknamed him 'Father Christmas' due to his long white

Upon prising it open, human remains were found inside.

beard. No one questioned the nature of their relationship, but assumptions were made that it was more than 'just friends'.

At the time of her disappearance, Betts had travelled to Philip Island with Coombs to the home of friend, Nicole Godfrey. Allegedly, in bed that night, the pair had argued, resulting in Coombs placing Betts in a 'sleeper hold' and a 'figure-four-headlock' before strangling her until she died.

The court went on to hear that Coombs then gathered some cord and a box of knives from his car, then carried Betts' body to the bathroom, placing her in a tub and tying her feet to the taps. He then became a veritable 'butcher', dismembering the corpse and placing her arms, legs, head and torso in plastic bags. Finding the task 'too difficult', Coombs took a sleep before going on to finish the job.

...he cut open the bags and threw the body parts into the sea...

The gory task completed, he drove the massacred Betts to Newhaven Beach. Once there, he cut open the bags and threw the body parts into the sea, slicing the abdomen of the torso to release stomach gases so as to prevent it floating to the surface.

The evil butcher clearly knew exactly what he was doing in this heinous disposal of the body and his efforts to ensure it would never be found.

Three others appeared in court with Coombs.

Nicole Godfrey, 26, was charged with being an accessory to the fact (and on a count of drug trafficking), with evidence indicating she had supplied the bags and vehicle Coombs used in the body's disposal, and possibly even offered more assistance. It is also alleged that she and Coombs were lovers…an association that continued after Betts' murder.

Also appearing were Maureen Renwick, 55, and Ryan Buscema, 25, both charged with attempting to pervert the course of justice and conspiracy to pervert the course of justice.

As Rachael Betts' family watched on, Magistrate Simon Garnett scheduled all four to reappear in court in February 2010, refusing an application for bail for Godfrey, posing her as a flight risk.

While the case is still to be heard, at least for the family of Rachael Betts, there is some movement towards justice over the murder of a young woman who, despite getting caught up with the 'wrong crowd', did not deserve to die in such a callous and brutal way.

It is also alleged that she and Coombs were lovers…

CHAPTER 3

THE FOLLY OF YOUTH

BRANDED FOR LIFE

Rebecca Mendoza, from the talented Mendoza family, seemingly had the world at her feet.

She had been working her way up in the world of entertainment, with successive roles in big productions such as *Les Miserables* and *Miss Saigon*.

While performing, she met Marlon Brand, a Canadian import, with who she fell madly in love. They became yet another 'showbiz couple', matching up with her sister Natalie who was with the son of Jimmy Barnes, David Campbell.

Brand and Mendoza married and had a child—a daughter they named Phoenix. This joyous birth, however, could not save a faltering relationship between them.

The situation was made all the more painful for Brand because during this time he and Mendoza were cast mates in a production of *Showboat*, meaning he had to share a stage with her nearly every night of the week as their relationship crumbled horribly around them.

On 25 January 1999, Brand turned up at Mendoza's home in Melbourne on the pretext of wanting to discuss their failing marriage.

Instead, before any meaningful discussion could begin, he revealed a knife. In one agonising thrust, he stabbed Mendoza with such vengeance that he severed more than 70 per cent of her aorta as he twisted the knife deep inside her.

Brand fled.

The bleeding woman was rushed to hospital, where doctors rushed to save her life.

According to Mendoza,

'The doctors predicted I would have had a massive stroke because of the blood loss and thought, if I survived, I would probably be a vegetable.'

Placed on life-support, she was kept alive but, due to the severity of her injuries, doctors told her parents she would in all likelihood awaken brain-dead, if at all.

To everyone's amazement and happiness, after four days on life support she slowly began to regain consciousness. As doctors predicted, she had suffered a stroke which damaged her right side heavily, leaving her with a limp right arm and facing months of rehabilitation.

...before any meaningful discussion could begin, he revealed a knife.

But, she was alive, and that counted for more than anything.

Brand was not so lucky and, unlike the musicals the couple had lived their lives performing in, there was to be no happy ending for him.

Having fled the scene, one can only assume that the horror of what he had done all too soon caught up with Brand, remorse and guilt pushing him into a dark place.

The morning after the stabbing, as Mendoza fought for her life, he ended his.

Police found him hanging from a tree near a public toilet. Not far from his body was the knife he had used to stab the woman he supposedly love and could not live without.

A true crime of passion, albeit one with a more tragic ending for its perpetrator than its victim.

Police found him hanging from a tree near a public toilet.

VENGEFUL TEEN

Adolescence can be a troublesome time, bringing with it all manner of changes—physically, emotionally and otherwise.

When first love is thrown into the mix, even more potential confusion and drama can arise, with dramatic consequences.

Mark Zimmer would learn this lesson, and pay with his life.

Nineteen-year-old Mark Zimmer would learn this lesson, and pay with his life.

The two-year relationship of 17-year-old Nicola Martin and 18-year-old Leon Borthwick had been over for several months, at least according to Martin. She had told people she thought he was lazy and was concerned she was losing friends because of him being in her life.

Borthwick was reportedly not happy with this, even less so when Martin struck up a friendship with Zimmer, who acted as something of a knight in shining armour after the breakdown of her relationship with Borthwick.

Fearing he was being displaced, with no chance of getting Martin back, Borthwick needed to let Zimmer know exactly where he stood, doing so with a variety of threatening language and actions.

Still in contact with Borthwick on a somewhat frequent basis, Martin herself heard him threaten Zimmer, although never in a violent fashion. However, Borthwick's jealousy was beginning to boil over. At one point, friends of Zimmer's allege Borthwick pulled a knife on Zimmer, held it to his genitals and threatened to kill him.

Nicola was not making things any easier.

She continued to see Borthwick, despite their relationship being over and knowing of his animosity towards Zimmer, and had told him she still loved him in text messages. Friends had even seen them out together shopping, looking clearly affectionate.

Complicating the matter was the fact that Zimmer and Martin were more than 'just friends', despite what she was telling people to the contrary. Borthwick's instincts were right—Zimmer was indeed a real rival for Martin's affections, although, sensing more trouble brewing, he was trying to extricate himself from the situation.

On 15 November 2008, the pressure in Borthwick's heart grew too much to bear. After a period of ongoing tension between them, Zimmer and Borthwick organised their respective groups of friends to support them for yet another confrontation, and things looked like they were going to get ugly. The group supporting Zimmer allegedly armed itself with tools, including spanners and window clean-

Borthwick pulled a knife on Zimmer, held it to his genitals and threatened to kill him.

ers, something friends of Zimmer's would later deny, saying it was meant to be a friendly meeting.

When Borthwick did not appear at the designated meeting spot, Zimmer and his group decided to go find him, heading for his home in Ormond Rd, Narre Warren. Zimmer's father accompanied them, possibly hoping to be the voice of reason and to help put an end to the animosity.

As they waited in the middle of the road just after midnight on 16 November, Borthwick chose his moment to arrive—behind the wheel of a Tarrago van.

...sending him flying through the air almost 20 meters...

Driving on the wrong side of the road, he aimed himself at Zimmer, hitting him and sending him flying through the air almost 20 meters to the next house. Borthwick fled the scene while Zimmer, despite desperate efforts to resuscitate him, died in his father's arms.

Homicide squad detectives tracked down Borthwick, finding several panels damaged on the car, and he appeared in an out-of-sessions hearing at the Melbourne Custody Centre later that night, where he was refused bail and later charged with murder.

In March 2009, Borthwick's defence counsel Patrick Doyle applied for bail, telling the Victorian Supreme Court that a trial date could be two years away and, if granted bail, Borthwick would live with his parents and surrender his passport. Justice Cummins approved bail on very strict grounds, in particular addressing concerns by the prosecution that associates of Borthwick had possibly been threatening potential witnesses.

Borthwick is now free on bail, awaiting his committal hearing, which was initially scheduled for November 2009, but as yet has not occurred. He is likely to go to trial sometime in late 2010.

Borthwick is now free on bail, awaiting his committal hearing...

YOUNG LOVE GONE SOUR

Just days before her 19th birthday, on New Years Eve, with 2008 about to begin, Amaranta Vega was on top of the world.

Nicknamed 'Amma', the young woman was piecing together the life she wanted.

Within a month, she would be a qualified childcare worker and, not long after, her delighted father was going to send her on an all-expenses-paid overseas trip. Upon her return, the family planned to buy a childcare centre, which she and her mother would operate.

The icing on the cake?

A boyfriend of two and a half years, 22-year-old Wayne Antoniazzo, with who she was infatuated, something her family didn't wholly approve of, but nor would interfere with.

Unfortunately, for Amma, this seemingly bright future and happy life were abruptly about to come to an end.

Wayne and Amma had decided to head down from Campbelltown to Canberra to visit family for New Years Eve. What should have been a night of celebration turned sour when a jealous Amma rounded on her boyfriend, accusing him of looking at another girl at the party.

This led to a quarrel mildly physical at times and loud enough for neighbours to come

What should have been a night of celebration turned sour...

out into the street to see what was going on, and to call police.

What happened next was the stuff of nightmares.

Antoniazzo rifled through Vega's handbag, fished out her car keys and drove off. Following his departure, either out of frustration or despair or for some other reason we will now never know, Vega lay down on the road.

Onlookers to this late-night drama debated whether to go and check on her, but before they could, Vega's own car, driven by Antoniazzo, returned at high speed around a corner, back towards where his girlfriend was on the ground, no doubt unaware she lay there on the road.

One witness said,

'She saw the car coming, she lifted her head up, but it was too fast for her to get out of the way. It was too close for him to slow down.'

After the car allegedly hit the woman with a loud bang, the driver sped off.

Police arrived at the scene to find Vega curled up in a ball, a pool of blood around her head. Ambulance crews arrived soon after, by which time she had lost a litre of blood. Paramedics attempted to revive her—she was suffering from severe facial injuries, uncontrollable bleeding, collapsed lungs, a fractured

After the car allegedly hit the woman with a loud bang, the driver sped off.

pelvis and a fractured femur.

Antoniazzo called Vega's phone not long after his disappearance, worried he had hit her. Her brother answered, telling him she was in an ambulance but seemed OK.

Vega was not 'OK'.

She died in hospital at 6.45 am.

Antoniazzo was found by police near the Federal Highway where he had slept that night after his car had run out of petrol and allegedly after calling friends to tell them to come get him. He immediately declared himself to them.

Taken in for questioning, when released from the watch house later he reportedly left saying,

'I killed my girlfriend. I'm sorry but it's just hit me what I've done.'

On 4 January, at a hearing at the ACT Magistrate's court, Antoniazzo pleaded not guilty to a charge of manslaughter and a second charge of failing to stop and give assistance. He admitted to other charges, including driving while disqualified and possessing a prohibited substance, and did not apply for bail.

In February 2008, the charge of manslaughter was upgraded to murder, but, to the dismay of Vega's family, he was granted bail, and later in August the charge was downgraded to manslaughter once more. On the final day of the committal hearing, Chief Magistrate Ron Cahill found there was enough evidence to commit Antoniazzo to trial, but said he was not satisfied there was enough evidence to commit him on a charge of murder.

Antoniazzo will now face the ACT Supreme Court on charges of manslaughter and failure to stop after an accident.

Despite vision tests performed by police that indicate Antoniazzo must have known Vega was lying on the road (regardless of Antoniazzo's complaints of poor eyesight), it remains to be seen whether the prosecution can prove he caused her death.

Antoniazzo must have known Vega was lying on the road...

CHAPTER 4

'BENT' PASSION

INNOCENT vs NOT GUILTY

'Please don't forget that "not guilty" does not mean "innocent".'

The father of 20-year-old Matthew Leveson uttered these emotional words after a court found his boyfriend, 46-year-old Michael Atkins, not guilty of Matthew's murder, seemingly indicating he still held deep reservations about the decision.

Atkins and Leveson had first met in 2006 at an Oxford St nightclub, Stonewall, in the gay heart of Sydney. They had struck up a friendship by text message as Atkins was living in Newcastle at the time, and the men eventually became live-in lovers.

On the night of 23 September 2007, the couple visited the Darlinghurst nightclub, Arq. They reportedly left around 3.30am, the time Leveson's brother Peter last saw them. Two days later, when he did not turn up to his job at a call centre, Atkins and Leveson's parents reported him missing to police, with Atkins telling them he had seen him the day before in Cronulla.

Police went on to find Leveson's car on 25 September parked at Waratah Oval in Sutherland, a known gay sexual cruise area, just a short distance from his home. Someone had wiped all fingerprint marks from it, a receipt for tape and a mattock was found inside, and a sub-woofer was missing, later found in Atkins' garage.

It was immediately feared that Leveson was the victim of a gay hate-crime.

It was immediately feared that Leveson was the victim of a gay hate-crime.

The disappearance remained a mystery until August 2008 when police arrested Atkins for the murder after putting together a strong circumstantial case against him. Besides the discovery of the speaker in Atkins' garage, CCTV footage showed him buying the tape and mattock in a hardware store the day after Leveson's disappearance.

Atkins had also allegedly texted 'hey sexy' to another man the day Leveson had last been seen, a sign of him straying from the relationship. A workmate of Leveson's went on to confirm this, giving evidence that before he went missing Leveson had complained to her about Atkins wanting threesomes and thinking he was 'God's gift to men', implying things were not going so well with their relationship. The witness went on to imply that Leveson had suggested some physical aggression had come into play during the couple's discussion when Leveson refused to open up their relationship.

In court, Mr Maxwell, for the prosecution, contended Atkins had killed his lover some time on Sunday morning. He had then bought the mattock to dig a grave and used the tape to wrap the body, which, after removing the sub woofer, he put it in the boot. He was accused of then hiding the body and dumping the car where it would later be found.

Defence barrister Keith Chapple posed a vastly different scenario.

Referring to evidence that the couple had sold drugs at ARQ, he suggested Leveson might easily have met with foul play at the hands of a drug supplier or succumbed to the effects of an accidental overdose while 'testing' a new product. There was also the possibility that it had been a hate crime, as originally mooted, or that Leveson was in fact still alive and had simply left his boyfriend, disappearing in the same way he briefly had when he met Atkins in 2006 and had not told his family where he was.

On 20 October 2009, a New South Wales Supreme Court jury found Atkins not guilty of murdering Leveson, also finding him not

He had then bought the mattock to dig a grave and used the tape to wrap the body...

guilty of manslaughter.

After the court brought down the verdict, the distraught Leveson family, stunned by the decision, appealed for any information as to the whereabouts of their son. Despite a deep abiding love for Matthew, his father's strong words and the need for some kind of closure, unless some compelling new evidence emerges, there is little chance for an appeal.

Matthew Leveson and Michael Atkins

ACCIDENTAL OR INTENTIONAL?

The most innocent of items can become weapons of destruction.

In the case of a gay couple, Trent Chen* and Fabio Culotto*, a lover's tiff would end with a deathblow from a juicer.

They had lived in their jointly owned flat in the inner south Sydney suburb of Alexandria since 2004 when Culotto brought the $600K property. The 23 year age difference between them—Chen was 49 with Culotto his senior at 72—had for the most not seemed to bother the couple, but in recent times Chen had allegedly voiced concerns to friends that he was considering ending the relationship.

And, end it did, on Easter Saturday, 7 April 2007, albeit in a far from amicable way.

Sometime during Good Friday the couple had argued about a tradesman who was doing some tiling work, after which Chen stormed off. By the next morning, they had smoothed things over, allegedly engaging in consensual 'make-up' sex. While things may have seemed OK between them, clearly Culotto was still disturbed.

As Chen made carrot-juice for them, his lover brought the tradesmen issue up once more and yet another fight broke out.

...a lover's tiff would end with a deathblow from a juicer.

Later, a neighbour would say they heard a sound from the apartment, like a shelf falling, pots clanging and lids rolling around the floor. This was followed by a loud scream, which they thought might be singing at the time, and then dead silence for up to ten minutes.

The silence was eventually broken by the sound of wailing, prompting a phone call to the home. Chen answered, but was apparently hysterical.

At about 9.15am, the first witness arrived on the scene to find Chen wailing and crying hysterically, cradling Culotto's head, rocking back and forward, his arms extremely tightly bound around the deceased's neck and head.

By the time police and ambulance officers arrived, Culotto's heart had stopped and, despite attempts at resuscitation, he was declared dead.

Police took Chen into custody for questioning. Showing them a fresh 'Chinese burn' on his arm, he admitted they had been fighting and that Culotto had accidentally fallen down the stairs during the altercation.

The state of Culotto's body, and evidence from the crime scene, indicated this was not necessarily the case. Wounds sustained to the head would later be connected in an autopsy to the conclusion he had died from blunt force injuries to the head and neck—marks around

...Culotto's heart had stopped and, despite attempts at resuscitation, he was declared dead.

his neck were not unlike those received from strangulation.

Compounding such evidence, contrary to the notion of Culotto falling down the stairs, was the discovery of a bloodstained juice extractor bowl and spout near the body. Culotto's DNA was found on the spout of the juice extractor.

There was also further evidence that the juicer bowl had been thrown at the wall in the kitchen above the doorway, causing some damage. Fine blood sprays and some blood smudges were discovered around the staircase area, although paramedics may have left these while attending to the body. A detective at the scene also thought he noticed blood on the handle of a cleaning brush in the kitchen.

Fine blood sprays and some blood smudges were discovered around the staircase...

In May 2009, charged with both murder and the lesser conviction of manslaughter, Chen faced the court. He was acquitted on both counts, with Justice J Rothman deeming there to be too many gaps in the Crown's case as he directed the jury to acquit Chen.

Despite Chen's relief at being vindicated, the Department of Public Prosecution of NSW was not prepared to let the case go. In October 2009, they took the case to the Court of Appeals where Chief Justice James Spiegelman agreed that Justice Rothman had erred in his advice to the jury.

'(Justice Rothman) did not pay regard to the other facts to which the jury could have regard... the evidence of a fight, the absence of any other person on the premises, the time delay before contacting 000'.

While he affirmed the acquittal on the charge of murder, for which he still held there was little sign of premeditation, he quashed the manslaughter acquittal, ordering a new trial for the manslaughter charge.

*Names have been changed.

SECTION TWO:

UNSOLVED, UNPROVEN AND INNOCENT

*It is better to risk saving a guilty man
than to condemn an innocent one*

Voltaire

No matter how much time, money and effort go into some investigations, there will always be crimes that remain unsolved.

However, especially with improvements in the areas of investigative research and technology such as the use of DNA testing, these crimes may later be reopened as cold cases.

More frustrating than unsolved crimes, at least for authorities, are the crimes that remain unproven, even in the face of spectacular evidence that seemingly points to the obvious—that the prosecuted is indeed guilty.

In direct contrast, there are crimes where the prosecuted is desperate to clear their name of the charges laid before them, proclaiming innocence, sometimes right until their final dying breath.

CHAPTER 5

UNSOLVED OR UNPROVEN

HIS BROTHER'S KEEPER

Denis Tanner had witnessed the traumatic breakdown of his brother's first marriage.

Years later, the burly Victorian police officer feared that, Laurie was once more about to be emotionally devastated. He was of the belief that Jennifer, Laurie's second wife, was intending to walk away from their marriage. If the anticipated rejection ended up in the divorce courts again, the resulting drain on finances could well cost the Tanners the family farm.

We may never know the mindset or motives that underpinned Denis Tanner's reactions, but it would appear that a tragic outcome resulted from a real or imagined family crisis.

In November 1984, the 27-year-old wife and mother of a 21-month old baby was found dead in her armchair, with two bullet wounds to her head and through each

Jennifer Tanner

Laurie Tanner found the bloodied body of his wife slumped in an armchair...

hand, a classic sign of self defence.

A quarter of a century later, important unanswered questions about the controversial case remain hotly debated.

Did the young woman commit suicide?

Did Denis Tanner murder his sister-in-law?

Alternatively, was Tanner protecting the real culprit from punishment?

The basic facts about the fatality are not in dispute.

Laurie Tanner found the bloodied body of his wife slumped in an armchair, a rifle between her legs, in their home near the Victorian town of Bonnie Doon. His first priority was the welfare of his son. After ascertaining the baby boy was safe, he contacted a neighbour who telephoned the Mansfield police station. The officer-in-charge at Mansfield had signed in on his duty roster, but when the phone message regarding the death was received, he was 'unavailable'.

Consequently, two other officers assumed responsibility at the scene of the fatality. Neither was practised with attending the site of a shooting, but one of them Bill Kerr, despite his inexperience with crimes of this nature, felt some niggling suspicions from the word go.

After summoning a local doctor from a dinner party, they quickly examined the body and collectively decided the probable cause of death was suicide. By then, the missing senior officer was available, who supported the suicide theory and chose not attend the site.

Two days later, Dr Peter Dyte, the pathologist in charge of the autopsy in Melbourne, called it to a halt and contacted the Mansfield police station. He expressed his puzzlement to Sergeant Phipps that Tanner had two shots in her forehead as well as bullet wounds in her hands. In his view, the evidence before them indicated she had placed her hands defensively in front of her head before the shots were fired.

Furthermore, Jennifer Tanner's husband's .22 bolt-action rifle was lodged between her knees, the barrel aimed at her head, an awkward suicide method to adopt. Phipps quickly talked him around into believing otherwise, with an elaborate theory in which he posited that Tanner had held her hands over the end of the barrel while pushing the trigger with her toe. Dyte eventually came around to this theory, albeit reluctantly.

Other aspects of the investigation were also questionable.

The fact that the senior officer on the night of the crime did not travel to the crime scene, or bother to take fingerprints or photographs in the room where the woman's life

.22 bolt-action rifle was lodged between her knees, the barrel aimed at her head...

Jennifer Tanner's fear of guns was well known...

ended, was slipshod, hinting at either incompetence or possibly complicity. Bill Kerr felt uneasy about the investigation and, following his niggling doubts from attending on the night, was sceptical about the suicide assessment. Jennifer Tanner's fear of guns was well known, she was responsible for the welfare of her young baby in the house and she left no suicide note. Even small, seemingly insignificant details before the fatality occurred, such as Mrs. Tanner reportedly asking her husband to buy milk, a local paper and a cherry ripe chocolate bar for her when he went into town pointed towards her death being at someone else's hand and not a planned suicide.

Overall, there appeared to be nothing obvious in Jennifer Tanner's demeanour or character to suggest she was about to, or in fact would ever, take her own life. If anything, facts continued to mount to indicate the exact opposite. Perhaps the most damning piece of evidence, yet the one overlooked, was the deposition of Roslyn Smith, close friend of Jennifer Tanner.

Smith had taken a call three weeks prior to Tanner's death, during which Jennifer related being disturbed by the appearance of Dennis Tanner on her back doorstep. He told her he'd fought with his wife and was off to cool down, but wanted Laurie Tanner's .22 rifle.

After fetching the gun her brother-in-law took it and loaded it, then proceeded to follow her around the house, questioning whether she intended leaving his brother, which she vehemently denied was a possibility.

Before he left, Denis warned her not to mention this to her brother, but she did regardless.

Strangely, when cross-examined at the inquest, Laurie's recollection of the conversation was much reduced from Smith's recollection of what Jennifer Tanner had told her, and the seemingly crucial statement was dismissed. In the absence of any clear evidence, the hearing ended with an open finding handed down.

Bill Kerr, however, doggedly pursued some of the unsatisfactory aspects of the Tanner case. He lobbied for the rifle used to be tested by experts, but his request was deemed 'unnecessary'. He then proceeded through 'the proper channels' on the matter, which also produced a negative response. When Constable Kerr persuaded a close friend of the deceased to inform senior officers that Jennifer Tanner had never been in a suicidal frame of mind, he was sharply rebuked.

This new development, Kerr was told, should have been initiated in accordance with proper chain of command procedures. Kerr

After fetching the gun her brother-in-law took it and loaded it...

was frustrated by the continual incompetence or cover-ups he seemed to encounter. He felt ostracised by many of his colleagues, so he soon left the district and, not long after, the disillusioned man resigned from the police force.

Kerr's persistent doubts, however, were followed up by some elements of the media, leading to Dennis Tanner being scrutinised more closely. It emerged that he provided conflicting alibis on the night his sister-in-law died. He declared he attended a trotting meeting that evening, but another source of information placed him at a Bingo night function in the Melbourne suburb of Middle Park.

Then, in July 1995, a decade after Jennifer Tanner died, Bonnie Doon shot into the media spotlight again after the remains of Adele Bailey were found in an abandoned mine shaft about 200 metres from the Tanner family's former property. The transvestite prostitute had vanished from St Kilda when Denis Tanner was stationed in that suburb of Melbourne. Furthermore, the last entries in Bailey's case file were written by Tanner and a female officer, who later became his wife.

...the old Tanner homestead burnt to the ground under highly suspicious circumstances.

After Adele Bailey's remains were uncovered, the old Tanner homestead burnt to the ground under highly suspicious circumstances. The house had been deserted since Laurie Tanner and his son had shifted to Mansfield to live with Tanner's parents. The electricity to the homestead had long been disconnected and it appeared likely that the very hot blaze was fuelled by burnt paper. As the fire took hold that night, a passing truck driver reported seeing a person near the burning building.

Effectively, the burning of the Tanner farmhouse hindered further forensic investigations. Denis Tanner, by then a senior police officer at nearby Benalla, sought no involvement in the Bailey homicide case and the issue was left in limbo. However, the mysterious house fire ignited renewed interest in the Jennifer Tanner case.

The late woman's cousin was a serving police officer who had long held suspicions about the suicide theory. He confided his doubts to a trusted senior police officer, resulting in the cold case Tanner file being re-examined. Because of the senior task force's thorough re-examination of the evidence, the findings of the original inquest were quashed.

In 1998, the Victorian State Coroner, Graeme Johnstone, headed a new inquiry. By the end of the 23-day hearing, the extent of police cronyism, bungling and potential cover-ups was clearly exposed, with Denis Tanner named by the coroner as the person who shot and killed Jennifer Tanner. The accused maintained his innocence, choosing not to

... a passing truck driver reported seeing a person near the burning building.

...Denis Tanner would not be charged with Jennifer Tanner's murder.

give evidence at the inquest on the grounds of self-incrimination.

In 1999, the Office of Public Prosecutions decided that 'on the evidence currently available', Denis Tanner would not be charged with Jennifer Tanner's murder. Suspended from duties during the investigation, once exonerated, Tanner resigned from the Force.

The Tanner case re-emerged, if in a slightly different form, once more in July 2009. Detective Inspector Paul Newman and Senior Sergeant Martin Allison had used dubious evidence, obtained from a psychic, to convince a High Court judge that listening devices should be installed in Denis Tanner's home to allow the gathering of further vital evidence. They were charged with 'disgraceful conduct' after attempting to 'dishonestly strengthen' their case against Denis Tanner for the alleged murder of Adele Bailey. The Victorian Office of Public Prosecutions rejected the recommendation to pursue criminal charges against the men and the case was dropped.

MURDER NOT SO
BLACK AND WHITE

Phillip Island, on Victoria's Westernport Bay, is a popular holiday destination, famous for its daily 'Penguin Parade'. Half a million tourists each year come to watch the tiny black and white creatures, the Little Penguins, emerge from the ocean at dusk each night and feed their young with fish harvested from Bass Strait.

It is difficult to imagine violence intruding on the peaceful tranquillity of island life. However, the combination of a brutal murder (still unsolved 23 years after the body was discovered) and the mystery disappearance of a prime suspect have left a smear on the island's untarnished, peaceful atmosphere.

On 22 September 1986, the battered body of 23-year-old Beth Barnard was found on her bedroom floor at the Rhyll farmhouse where she lived, savagely knifed to death. Shortly after, the car belonging to Vivienne Cameron was discovered abandoned near the bridge connecting the island to the mainland town of San Remo.

The connection?

Cameron was the wife of Barnard's lover, Fergus Cameron.

Fergus and Beth became friends, and later

...Beth Barnard was found on her bedroom floor at the Rhyll farmhouse where she lived...

lovers, while employed at the Phillip Island Penguin Parade. Barnard also worked as a farm worker on Cameron's property, helping further cement their relationship.

Shortly before her death, Beth confided to her two close friends that she loved Fergus, but that she was loath to break up a closely-knit family, which included two young sons.

Fergus Cameron allegedly viewed the problem differently.

He claimed that, shortly before Barnard was murdered, his wife had agreed to move to Melbourne and allow Beth Barnard and him to have custody of the two children. Friends of Vivienne remain sceptical about this assertion.

'She was very fond of her children,' recalled one, 'and the last person you'd expect to kill someone.'

Vivienne Cameron was regarded by many as a quiet achiever, seemingly at odds with her husband's claim that she attacked him viciously on more than one occasion because of his infidelity. In fact, on the very night Barnard was murdered, she allegedly cut his ear so badly with a broken wine glass that the wound required stitching at the local hospital.

The unfaithful husband maintained he never defended himself from these alleged attacks, also stating that before the wine glass

...she allegedly cut his ear so badly with a broken wine glass that the wound required stitching at the local hospital.

attack he had disclosed details to his wife about his sexual relationship with Beth Barnard. After the assault, an apparently remorseful Vivienne Cameron drove her husband to the hospital for medical attention before arranging for him to stay at her married sister's home for the night. Leaving him safely there, she drove away.

And was never seen again.

If Vivienne Cameron viciously murdered Beth Barnard later that night, she certainly displayed unexpected strength. Barnard's throat was deeply cut to the neck bone and a letter resembling the capital 'A' was carved into her chest. Police subsequently believed that the investigation of the crime scene was conducted with undue haste and criticised the fact that it took a further four weeks before bloodstained evidence was analysed.

Sergeant Geoff Frost later directed an unsuccessful four-day search for Mrs. Cameron's body in Westernport Bay near where her abandoned car was discovered. He remains unconvinced that the woman committed suicide there. No body or other evidence was found and the reportedly devoted mother left no explanatory note. In her will, she conventionally bequeathed her assets to her husband and children.

Furthermore, Frost believed that if foul

...throat was deeply cut to the neck bone and a letter resembling the capital 'A' was carved into her chest.

...women attackers almost invariably attack their male partner, rather than his lover.

play had occurred, expert police divers would have found some trace of Vivienne Cameron's remains in the water. It should be noted, however, that there are other examples of drowning in this area where no evidence of the missing victims has ever been discovered.

Other unconvinced observers have pointed out that in these kinds of scenarios women attackers almost invariably attack their male partner, rather than his lover.

There is also a particular piece of evidence from a local woman difficult to dismiss. Gillian Fraser steadfastly maintains she received a social phone call from the missing woman four hours after police divers began their search for Cameron's body. She remembers discussing patchwork dolls with her, but this evidence, from a reportedly rational and reliable person, was apparently not relevant to the local coroner as no mention was made of this intriguing development at the 1987 hearing.

During this traumatic September 1986 tragedy, the reactions of Fergus Cameron were worthy of note—the man who had lost a lover (and possibly a wife) appeared to be relatively unfazed by the violent episode. Investigating officers found him to be so outwardly cool, calm and collected, they wondered if sedatives were affecting his behaviour.

A letter sent by Barnard, but not received

by a London friend until after the murder, may also be relevant. In the correspondence, Barnard asked if she could join her friend for a holiday in the U.K, disclosing she wished to leave Phillip Island to remove herself from a messy affair that could potentially bring much suffering to the two Cameron children.

At a hearing in Korumburra on 20 August 1987, the coroner submitted that, after contributing to Beth Barnard's death, Cameron took her own life by plunging from the high bridge to the dangerous waters below.

...Cameron took her own life by plunging from the high bridge to the dangerous waters below.

This is still a commonly held belief and finding which effectively closed the case.

Vivienne Cameron's disappearance, however, was never adequately explained, and her body never discovered.

A 'MUD'DLED INVESTIGATION

On 25 June 1991, the body of Nancy King was found face down in a water-filled pit on her Tallygaroopna farm near Shepparton.

The cause of death?

Mrs King had hit her head either when she tripped and fell...

Most believed Mrs King had hit her head either when she tripped and fell, or when cattle knocked her into the pit.

However, her eldest son, Jason King, persistently pressured local police to investigate further.

Sixteen years later, the courage of his convictions finally led to the reopening of the cold case, with police charging the dead woman's husband, ex-VFL football player Graeme King, with his wife's murder.

Jason (and others) were sceptical from day one about aspects of Nancy King's death. For years, she was subject to both physical and emotional abuse from her husband, and close family members believed she planned to leave the marriage. Jason knew this without a doubt—just prior to her death, his mother confided in him that she planned to use a $60 000 payout from a car accident to flee the abusive relationship.

After the discovery of his mother's body, Jason was shocked to read a solicitor's letter urging his father to organise an inquest as soon as possible. Several weeks before his wife's demise, King senior had insured her life for $100 000. and after her death his solicitor urged the debt-plagued farmer to gain access to the life insurance payout quickly.

In terms of her physical state, medical experts reported she suffered 16 bruises and abrasions, too many to have been inflicted in a simple fall. In particular, one severe blow to the head was considered possibly sufficient to stun the victim before she died. The pathologist judged that the bruise on the forehead came from a blow perhaps hard enough to knock the victim unconscious, but not hard enough to kill.

There also lay the simple (and seemingly damning) evidence that police found no mud on the dead woman's gumboots, despite the ground near the pit being soggy. To add to this, the clothes on the corpse were not the usual garments Nancy King wore while working on the farm.

After Jason King expressed his misgivings about the death to police, they advised him to secretly tape any conversations he might have with his father about the tragedy. Despite this, detectives soon concluded there was insufficient evidence to charge Graeme King and the death was described as a case of 'accidental drowning.'

Nancy King

...police found no mud on the dead woman's gumboots...

Graeme King

...the bruises and abrasions found on the drowned corpse...

Shelley Robinson, the coroner assigned to the case, was surprised by the police decision. Troubled by the bruises and abrasions found on the drowned corpse, she was relieved when the Melbourne homicide squad re-opened the cold case in 2005.

Graeme King's four children, along with the Graeme King's four brothers and many local acquaintances, were never convinced Nancy King's death was accidental—doubts which appeared vindicated when dramatic new evidence surfaced.

At a hearing in 2007, Susan Molnar, a former tabletop dancer at Shepparton's Club Rawhide, released startling details about an alleged conversation she had with Graeme King on the club premises in 2000. While performing a lap dance for a customer, she conveyed her condolences about his wife's death and received a reply she was not expecting.

'I hated her, I killed her.'

On that same night, Molnar informed a male workmate about King's revelations, pointing him out. The colleague confirmed the man as 'Kingy' whose wife had died a few years ago.

King denied ever making such a comment and insisted he loved his wife and did not murder her. The jury was unable to come to a unanimous verdict and the case was dismissed.

But the case was not yet over.

In November 2008, after a two-week trial in Victoria's Supreme Court, King was finally acquitted of murder. Graeme King's lawyer, Howard Mason, maintained the decision to prosecute King was based on a ludicrous theory built up over years of baseless community gossip, rumour and innuendo. Jason King's legal representative, Ian Cuncliffe, acknowledged that the prosecution was unable to prove beyond reasonable doubt that Mrs. King had been murdered, and blamed an 'appalling' 1991 police investigation on the eventual outcome.

'The Keystone Cops couldn't have done a worse job of investigation at that time,' Cuncliffe later lamented.

After walking away a free man, the defendant expressed his wish to reconcile with his four children, but Jason King flatly rejected this possibility.

'He's dreaming,' said the now 35-year-old Sydney sign writer. 'He won't see us, he won't see his grandkids, and he's going to be a very lonely man.'

'...he won't see his grandkids, and he's going to be a very lonely man.'

DEATH IN THE 'BURBS

Michael Griffey

...the place smelled terrible, like rotting meat.

A day after the New Year in 2006, 45-year-old, millionaire entrepreneur Michael Griffey was found bludgeoned to death in his garage in the outer Melbourne suburb of Pakenham. He had sustained head injuries, delivered by a blunt metal object.

His daughter Cassandra and estranged wife Diane entered the garage on 2 January. Immediately, Cassandra noticed the lights were already on and that the place smelled terrible, like rotting meat. It was then that she saw the blankets covered in blood and her dad's sunglasses at one end of the blankets, his thongs at the other.

When police arrived to examine the murder scene to witness Griffey's body tacked to the concrete floor in a pool of dried blood (indicating he had been dead for several days), their thoughts must have turned to the likelihood of a crime of passion.

This was not an entirely incredible assumption.

Not long before he was found, Griffey had joked to a friend he was worth more dead than alive to his estranged wife when he had spoken to him about money problems he had been having with her. A bank account that should have been in the black was in fact $180 000 in the red, with Griffey suspecting this to be the result of Diane's overspending.

The Griffey's had been separated since 2004, but, despite Michael being involved with other women, had maintained a sexual relationship.

In fact, police even believed they might have had sex on the day of his murder.

In February 2006, Diane was charged with murder, but released on bail as the judge felt the case lacked any hard evidence and that it would take anywhere up to two years before it came before the courts. Being released on bail would allow her to maintain the family business in the meantime, which might fail otherwise.

Some observers found this decision odd, especially when there was the possibility for great financial gain, of up to one million dollars, for Diane Griffey from the life insurance policies her husband had taken out—seemingly hard enough evidence to link her to the killing. There were also the rumours of the family business being in disarray, purportedly at the hands of Diane, which meant that the notion of her running the business in Michael's absence was a potential disaster.

The case did not come before the courts until January 2007, at which time the court reconfirmed that the prosecution's case still

...there was the possibility for great financial gain, of up to one million dollars...

lacked any hard evidence.

However, Magistrate Paul Smith had quite specific reasons for his unease about which direction the case should take. Griffey's son, Kenny, who had an argument with his father on the day of his death, was just as likely a suspect and yet although he had been originally arrested on suspicion at the time of the death, was released without further questioning.

Further supporting the unlikelihood of Diane being involved in the murder was the fact that she had held a New Years Eve party in the house right next to the garage where the body lay. Those who attended the party reported that Diane had seemed relaxed on the night, with no indication of any wrong doing so nearby.

There was also much conjecture about the time and place of death.

...neither a pathologist nor an entomologist working on the case could agree on the exact time of death.

A mobile phone message that initially helped police estimate Mr Griffey's time of death was later compromised after it was discovered that the deceased owned two or more such phones. Furthermore, neither a pathologist nor an entomologist working on the case could agree on the exact time of death. It was also significant that no murder weapon was found.

So, regardless of the still-shaky case presented by the Prosecution, Smith said that although he had difficulties with the case, he did not want to usurp the role of a jury. He ordered Diane Griffey to appear in the Victorian Supreme Court on 24 April for a directions hearing, which she did, with a court date set for October 2007.

Then came the twist no one could have expected.

In July, just a few months out from the court case, Cassandra Griffey admitted to police she had killed her father. When this was made public, on the eve of her mother's trial, a postponement was called so that police could follow new leads.

...Cassandra Griffey admitted to police she had killed her father.

Finally, on 13 November 2008, nearly three years after Michael Griffey was murdered, the case against Diane Griffey was dropped in the Supreme Court after prosecutors admitted that the Crown would not be able to prove who murdered the millionaire businessman. Dianne Griffey's trial was aborted and her defence lawyer, Chris Dane, declared his client should never have faced trial on the evidence presented.

Latest reports indicate that the Griffey homicide case is now in the hands of cold case investigators. It is possible that a culprit, or culprits, could still be charged with murder in the future if new evidence surfaces because no one has faced trial yet for the crime.

CHAPTER 6

INNOCENT

THE GUN ALLEY MURDER

It took 86 years for justice to prevail, but on 28 May 2008, Colin Campbell Ross was finally found not guilty of murdering a 12-year-old girl in Melbourne on New Year's Eve 1921, becoming the first Victorian to be posthumously pardoned.

Closure in the case might have occurred as early as August 1964, when 75-year-old Ivy Irene Matthews (aka Ivy Chollet) lay dying in an East Melbourne hospital. However, this key witness in the 1922 'Gun Alley' case divulged nothing further about the murder that resulted in the wrongful execution of Colin Ross.

On 31 December 1921, a bottle collector discovered the naked, raped and strangled body of a young girl in Gun Alley, just off Little Collins Street, in the Melbourne CBD. She was identified as 12-year-old Alma Tirtschke who no one had seen since the previous afternoon when she set off on an errand for her grandmother. The press, notably the *Herald*, led public calls to find the killer, putting pressure on police to quickly solve the murder.

Under mounting pressure, police investigators soon centred their attention on Colin Campbell Ross.

The man had previously been charged with various offences and had been licensee of the Australian Wine Café in the Eastern Arcade, which had a less-than savoury reputation. Witnesses verified Ross as being near the crime scene at the time of the murder and when the suspect tried to defend himself by arguing many shady types who frequented a nearby brothel often lurked in the area, police were dismissive.

Witnesses verified Ross as being near the crime scene at the time of the murder...

He was subsequently arrested and charged with the girl's murder, his trial commencing on 10 January 1922. A 20-year-old prostitute, Olive Maddox, stated she saw the homicide victim in Ross's bar on that fateful Friday shortly before the murder took place. Ivy Matthews, another prostitute, and Julia Gibson, who worked as a fortune-teller under the name Madame Gurkha, both testified Ross had confessed the crime to them.

Circumstantial evidence against the accused continued to grow. Government analyst Charles Price adamantly declared that 27 golden red hairs, found on a blanket in the wine bar, definitely came from the head of the deceased.

Furthermore, when Ross was in remand, it was alleged he had confided to fellow inmate, Sydney John Harding that he had killed Alma Tirtschke. Harding's evidence seemed especially credible, despite the fact that he had previously been convicted for perjury. He was in Sydney when the murder took place, far away from most press coverage about the homicide, and yet provided a detailed account of Ross's reported confessed to him.

And in what appeared to be final, damning evidence, police found pieces of cloth near Ross's Footscray home, allegedly from the girl's clothing, and strands of hair found at his residence were judged to match hair samples from the victim's head.

Unfortunately for the accused, Ross's own behaviour in court did not help his case.

At first nonchalant, then pugnacious and finally angry, he protested his innocence until the end, declaring police had framed him. The weight of hearsay evidence and Ross's attitude proved to be decisive for the jury, which found him guilty of murder.

On 15 February 1922, he was sentenced to death, to which he proclaimed,

'My life has been sworn away by des-

...strands of hair found at his residence were judged to match hair samples from the victim's head.

perate people.'

Subsequent appeals to the Victorian Full Court and the Australian High Court failed and, after spending his final two hours with a minister of religion, Colin Campbell Ross was hung at 10 am on 24 April 1922 at Melbourne Gaol. In the space of a mere four months, a man had been charged, convicted and hanged for a crime of which he ardently argued he was innocent.

Although there was quite marked division of opinion on the Ross case, the defendant's consistent claims of innocence received as much support as derision. Ross's barrister, Thomas Brennan, in his book *Gun Alley Tragedy* attempted to establish that Ross had been hanged for a crime not of his doing, but this was not enough to instigate a re-examination of the case.

More recently, in 1993, another book on the case by Kevin Morgan, *Gun Alley: Murder, Lies and Failure of Justice,* also attempted to raise awareness about inadequacies in the Ross case. The testimony of six reliable witnesses was kept from the court, all of which placed Ross in the saloon during the time at which it was believed Tirtschke was murdered.

There was also the fact that, for any evidence resulting in a conviction, the government offered the large sum of one thousand

> **In the space of a mere four months, a man had been charged, convicted and hanged for a crime...**

pounds. From this generous reward, Ivy Matthews received 350 pounds; Sydney John Harding, 200 pounds; and Olive Maddox, 170 pounds. These witnesses were already considered of dubious character and the compensation they were awarded for the vital testimony provided, which there can be no doubt helped decide the guilty verdict, could have been a major incentive for them to provide falsely damning evidence.

Following a recent re-examination of the facts, it became obvious that key elements of the evidence mounted against Ross were seriously flawed. One major discrepancy was the credence paid to the strands of hair found at Ross's Footscray home. Morgan began a legal fight to have these submitted for DNA testing, the result of which led to the conclusion that they did not in fact belong to Tirtschke.

Consequently, in May 2008, Ross was offered a posthumous pardon, the first in Victoria's legal history.

The sad irony of the case is that the family of Alma Tirtschke long-held that Ross should be exonerated completely, believing her murderer may well have been a member of their own family. Unfortunately, for the wrongfully hanged Ross, the pardon and this belief of Alma's family, comes nearly a century too late.

...her murderer may well have been a member of their own family.

RUPERT MAXWELL STUART

Rupert Maxwell
Stuart

Rupert Maxwell Stuart came from a deprived background.

By the age of ten, the part-aboriginal boy, raised by the Aranda people, was working as a stockman. He spent the best part of the next two decades in a variety of labouring jobs located in outback Australia. At various country agricultural shows, 'Maxie' Stuart earned extra money in boxing rings. His sister taught him to write his name laboriously in block letters, the only brush with literacy he ever had.

A few days before Christmas in December 1958, 27-year-old Stuart arrived in the remote South Australia town of Ceduna with Gieseman's Fun Land Carnival, with who he was employed as a labourer.

That evening, Stuart and another carnival employee attended the local picture theatre and, after the movie ended, the drunken pair pestered a group of young local women, who managed to escape their unwanted attentions by catching a taxi.

...the drunken pair pestered a group of young local women...

Maxie was especially attracted to one of the women and the next morning unsuccessfully attempted to locate her in Ceduna. Frustrated at not being able to find her, the young man turned to alcohol to soothe his disappointment. By early afternoon, a resentful and drunken Maxie lurched towards the beach on his way back to work at Funland.

Late that same afternoon, nine-year-old Mary Olive Hattam was reported missing from the beach near Ceduna. A frantic search began and sadly, close to midnight, searchers found the body of the little girl in a cave near where she had been playing. She was bloodied and mangled, her face smashed in…and the small girl had been raped and murdered.

Police found nearby a large bloodstained rock they believed the weapon the killer had used when he fractured his young victim's skull. Black trackers later asserted that footprints found near the crime scene were those of an Aranda person and that these tracks led back to the Ceduna Township, straight to Max Stuart.

By 9.30pm, police had him in custody.

Stuart's interrogation by six officers was reportedly intense and violent, and the ordeal only ended after he had signed a written statement with his customary block letter signature, confessing to the murder.

At his first trial on 20 December 1959, Stuart denied the crime.

In his short verbal defence, he claimed police had harassed him into signing the confession. Trial proceedings became confused when the coroner assigned to the case pro-

She was bloodied and mangled, her face smashed in…

...police forced him into confessing due to his poor command of English.

vided mixed messages about the time of the actual murder and Stuart's defence argued that police forced him into confessing due to his poor command of English.

Regardless, Stuart was found guilty as charged, and sentenced to death.

When an application for appeal was denied, opinions about due process in the Stuart case began to divide Australians. Police adamantly maintained that the written confession was an accurate record of what Stuart had actually stated.

Father Thomas Dixon, a prison chaplain, publicly expressed scepticism about this claim.

The doubting priest had previously discussed the case with Stuart in the Aranda language. He was completely convinced that an illiterate, outback aboriginal could not have uttered the sophisticated language used in the written confession.

Despite Father Dixon's protests, a second appeal application failed and, after the Privy Council in London rejected a bid for a re-trial, the death sentence for Stuart appeared to be inevitable.

Fortunately for Maxie, crucial new evidence unexpectedly surfaced.

The Guiseman Fun Land Carnival group had been located near Mt. Isa and three employees confirmed that Stuart was working with or near them when the murder took place. By the time of this revelation, the Adelaide media was stridently vocal about the conduct of the case and the South Australian Premier Sir Thomas Playford bowed to public pressure, establishing a Royal Commission to fully reinvestigate all evidence.

Opposition about the troubled case remained after it was revealed that two of the three appointed commissioners had sat in previous review teams that rejected other appeals for Stuart. The Adelaide press trumpeted that the findings would be a farce and Stuart's legal representative resigned in disgust. As the hearing dragged on past 40 days, it was made known that the defendant had already been subjected to periods on death row on seven harrowing occasions. Although the commission findings came down concluding that Stuart's conviction was justified, authorities were persuaded to commute his death sentence to life imprisonment.

Max Stuart, rejected all his life by two widely different cultures, was finally released in 1973 on parole after serving 14 years.

Over the next ten years or so, he was imprisoned on and off for minor offences, before being released for the sixth and final time from Adelaide's Yatala Labour Prison.

...the defendant had already been subjected to periods on death row on seven harrowing occasions.

In 2002 a film about his case, *Black and White*, was released

Some good came of his time in custody as he improved his English language speaking ability, became literate, acquired work skills and developed a love of watercolour painting.

After his release in 1984, Stuart married and settled at Santa Theresa Mission near Alice Springs. He became an Aranda elder and during the late 1990s served as Chairman of the Central Land Council. In 2002 a film about his case, *Black and White*, was released starring Robert Carlyle, Colin Friels and Ben Mendehlson.

BRONIA ARMSTRONG'S FINAL STRUGGLE

Bronia Armstrong

'I did not kill Bronia Armstrong. My conscience is clear.'

These words were written on the suicide note penned by Reginald Spence Wingfield Brown before he hung himself in Brisbane's Boggo Road Prison just nine days after he was given a life sentence for the murder of a teenage girl.

...he hung himself in Brisbane's Boggo Road Prison just nine days after he was given a life sentence...

The 49-year-old manager of the Brisbane Associated Friendly Society (BAFS) Medical Institution was a typical, diligent white-collar worker of his generation. This was the same firm that employed 19-year-old Bronia Armstrong as a stenographer. The young woman had previously known Brown's daughter when they were students at the same secondary school.

When he became infatuated with Armstrong, the manager's customary conservative persona apparently altered significantly. Eventually, Armstrong was so offended by her employers embarrassing advances, she tended her resignation.

Unfortunately, this departure from her workplace came too late.

On 10 January 1947, just one week before she was due to leave, the ill-fated woman was strangled to death in the busy CBD section of the city during normal business hours. The cries she might have made while being possibly raped, then murdered, would have been disregarded by passersby, as the occasional scream was commonplace from patients undergoing medical procedures in the vicinity of the crime.

Her parents first became worried when Bronia failed to return home after work. Upon calling management, they were informed that their missing daughter had last been seen having an animated phone conversation with a boyfriend, and that she had not been sighted since.

Next morning, the asphyxiated body of Bronia Armstrong was found in the BAFS waiting room. Questioned by police, Brown claimed that a depressed Bronia often told him of her wish to commit suicide. He believed his claims were supported by the atomiser of ethyl chloride found near her body. This assertion was greeted with general disbelief by those who knew her as the energetic young woman appeared to be consistently happy about her life.

Police investigations soon centred on Brown when scuffmarks were observed on the carpeted area between his office and the waiting room where the corpse was discovered—

...depressed Bronia often told him of her wish to commit suicide.

possible evidence the body had been dragged from room to room. Bruises to his hands and knees, which Brown claimed came from an assault on his person, were consistent with those a person might sustain while sitting on someone's chest and trying to strangle them.

Clearly, despite his protestations of innocence, the evidence was mounting against Brown, and investigators began to put together a picture of what they believed had occurred. It was their belief that near closing time on the day of Armstrong's murder, Brown had lured her into his office and, when rebuffed in his advances, the man had become enraged, murdering her. Once staff vacated the premises for the day, he dragged her body across the carpet into the waiting room, setting up the apparent suicide scene.

Brisbane's locals were both horrified and fascinated to know that a young woman had been murdered during business hours in a busy area of the city, with the trial attracting much interest. Brown continued vehemently to deny culpability, but the jury was unimpressed with his presentation, handing down a guilty verdict.

Sentenced to life imprisonment, his reputation in tatters, Reginald Spence Wingfield Brown did not see out even two weeks of his sentence. His suicide, only nine days after his

...he dragged her body across the carpet into the waiting room, setting up the apparent suicide scene.

imprisonment, brought the Armstrong case back into the public eye, adding a further twist to the sad tale of her untimely demise.

SECTION THREE:

PROVOCATION

There are only about 20 murders a year in London and not all are serious-some are just husbands killing their wives.

G. H. Hatherill

While this quote (from a work of fiction) is clearly intended to elicit a laugh, what it alludes to—the notion of provocation—is far from funny.

As Professor Jenny Morgan, former Deputy Dean of Melbourne Law School observed:

'Dead women tell no tales, (but) they have tales told about them.'

And, one might add, would have tales to tell of the one who killed them had they still been alive to do so.

For many years, the defence of provocation has remained a means by which those guilty of a crime of passion, mostly men, could have their transgression downgraded from murder to the lesser crime of manslaughter.

Over time, as outdated notions of gender relationships and in particular that between a husband and wife were being challenged, it became increasingly obvious that this defence was potentially getting in the way of justice.

Opponents of the law protested it was unacceptable for guilty people to receive a reduced sentence if their main defence was that their sense of pride or honour was the catalyst for violence. They argued that there should be no leniency for violence towards others under any circumstances.

Furthermore, the law of provocation often favoured men, as women did not usually possess the physical strength to inflict violence on an adult male in close confrontational situations. And it can't be denied that on the surface the use of provocation offers the impression that the notion of 'good' and 'bad' women was still enshrined in legal proceedings—that crimes of passion inflicted by males were dealt with more sympathetically in courtroom decisions.

Thankfully, in the face of mounting criticism, provocation is now slowly being unwound as a defence, at least in certain Australian jurisdictions.

Unfortunately, such has come at a terrible price—the deaths of innocents, mostly women.

FAMILY HONOUR

In February 1981, 16-year-old Zerrin Dincer sat in her bedroom, having a heart to heart with her mother.

Without warning Kemalettin Dincer, her stepfather, entered the room and thrust a knife into the teenager's heart, fatally wounding and killing her.

Two months earlier, Zerrin and her sister had presented at Western General Hospital where they told a social worker their father had threatened and attacked them for talking to boys. The following morning, their mother, scratched and bruised, also arrived at the hospital claiming her husband had tried to strangle her, something a social worker witnessed and noted.

Zerrin, wanting to avoid repeat incidents of violence, moved into the house of her boyfriend, Tony Darby, and his mother. This of course inflamed her stepfather even more, who then assumed she was sleeping with Darby, an even greater disgrace to him and his family's honour.

Thus, Dincer took matters into his own hands, dispatching his stepdaughter with the thrust of a knife and upholding his precious honour at the expense of a young woman on the verge of an adulthood she would never know.

...their mother, scratched and bruised, also arrived at the hospital claiming her husband had tried to strangle her...

When apprehended, Dincer readily confessed to police.

'I thrust it (the knife) very hard to kill her, she disgraced my honour'.

Despite this clear admission of guilt, Dincer's defence, Colin Lovitt, argued Zerrin's relationship with her boyfriend had brought dishonour to the family and to her father's position in the community. That was why he 'lost control', drew a knife from his sock and killed her, the court was told.

> '**I thrust it (the knife) very hard to kill her, she disgraced my honour**'.

The Judge in the matter, Justice Lush, directed the jury to consider whether an ordinary Muslim man might lose control and kill his daughter upon learning she was potentially sexually active.

Surprisingly, the evidence of the social worker was never aired in court, and although Dincer was found guilty, it was for the lesser crime of manslaughter, incurring a mere four years imprisonment.

Despite the differences in cultural and religious beliefs between Dincer and the Australian legal system's idea of what is right and wrong, this short sentence seems a small price to pay for the slaying of an innocent, and was the beginning of the end for the provocation law in Victoria.

VICKY CLEARY

One of the most publicised provocation cases surrounded the death of the sister of Phil Cleary, former Federal MP for the Melbourne seat of Wills, author and prominent media personality.

Vicky Cleary

Twenty-five-year-old Vicky Cleary entered into a relationship with Peter Keogh in 1987, which degenerated over four years into an abusive, volatile situation from which she eventually tried to extricate herself.

One sunny winter's morning as Vicky arrived at the kindergarten where she was employed, two months after she had officially ended the relationship with Keogh, she found the enraged man waiting for her in the car park.

As Vicky parked her car, Keogh wrenched the door open, grabbed her car keys and threw them across the parking lot. He then dragged Cleary from her car, with the terrified woman screaming for help, before viciously stabbing her. As he departed the scene, he callously wiped his knife clean before horrified onlookers, with Vicki barely clinging to life.

Her tenuous grip would soon falter— Vicky Cleary died several hours later.

When the case reached the courts, the killer's defence argued he allegedly suffered a

He then dragged Cleary from her car, with the terrified woman screaming for help...

Peter Keogh

**...he had only
killed her in
a moment
of loss of
self-control...**

personality disorder, and was thus unable to cope with rejection. In light of this, Justice Hampel instructed the jury they could consider a defence of provocation on the grounds that Keogh's intention was merely to slash Vicki Cleary's tires, and that he had only killed her in a moment of loss of self-control where an ordinary man might have been provoked in the same way.

Keogh was sentenced to eight years when the jury brought down a verdict of manslaughter, with a minimum parole period of six years, much to the distress of the Cleary family.

The only good to come of Vicki's death was the passion with which Phil Cleary with became infused in the quest to see such injustice could not occur in the future.

Over the proceeding years, he used all his influence as an MP and media commentator to comment where possible about the provocation law and to see it removed as a defence—an honourable mission, of which he would eventually see the fruits.

DOUBLE STANDARDS

Sometime in 1991, Heather Osland decided she could no longer stand her intolerable existence.

Heather Osland

For thirteen years, she had endured ongoing sexual, emotional and physical torment from her husband, Frank. The four children she had brought with her into the marriage were also under constant threat. The list of terror and torment he had perpetrated while married to her bordered on sadistic—the twisted man had shot a family pet in front of them, broken Heather's daughter's nose, cut her son's mouth to shreds when he smashed him in the head while he was wearing braces and had held Heather under water for filling the bath too much. He had also subjected her to sexual acts on a continuing basis, causing infections leading to her hospitalisation.

...held Heather under water for filling the bath too much...

He even removed fuses from the fuse-box when he left the house, leaving the family without power. Anything to upset and terrorise Heather and her children.

Sadly, despite police being called to the house on several occasions, no relief was in sight for the family, with no serious investigations of any of her claims ever occurring, despite word around town of the abuse.

Pushed to her absolute limit, rather than

taking her own life in despair as could easily have occurred, the Bendigo grandmother decided instead to end the life of the man who had subjected her to such suffering. The violence was now escalating to the point where Osland ordered Heather's eldest son David from the house, threatening to kill him. David considered this, but would not leave in fear of his mother's life.

...David slammed a length of pipe against his stepfather's head...

On 31 July 1991, Heather drugged her husband's food to sedate him, after which David slammed a length of pipe against his stepfather's head—a determined and fatal blow. The pair took his body to an alleged pre-prepared grave and buried him.

For the next three and a half years, the family lived free of his terror, but this peace would not last. One evening, after returning from visiting her father's grave on the fifteenth anniversary of his death, she was visited by local police who questioned her then charged Heather Osland with the murder of her husband.

When the case came before the courts, the jury found her guilty of murder, despite Osland's legal team invoking the defences of provocation and self-defence. This same jury was unable to reach a verdict on her co-accused, despite her son being the one who had allegedly inflicted the fatal blow. (At a later retrial, a new jury found him not guilty of either murder or manslaughter after he said he acted in self-defence of himself and his mother.)

In his sentencing remarks in 1996, Justice John Hedigan said that,

'Whilst Frank Osland was a cruel and violent man, his life nevertheless had value and the taking of it was a fully premeditated act done by you to turn your life around and preserve your situation.'

He sentenced Osland to fourteen-and-a-half years' jail, setting the non-parole period at nine-and-a-half years. She appealed the decision all the way to the High Court where a majority sustained both the verdict and sentence.

Justice Michael Kirby, who was in the majority, noted that battered woman syndrome,

'...is not a universally accepted and empirically established scientific phenomenon. Least of all does the raising of it cast a protective cloak over an accused charged with homicide.'

He went on to describe Heather Osland's attack as being 'coolly premeditated'.

During her ten years in prison, Heather continued to fight for justice, finally being released on 22 July 2005. At this time, she

...a new jury found him not guilty of either murder or manslaughter...

began a legal fight to obtain documents relating to her case and a plea of clemency as a means of understanding why such was refused by the government of the day.

This battle ended in May 2007 when the Court of Appeals ruled in favour of the Bracks' government's appeal to prevent the release of these documents. Osland appealed once more, this time to the High Court, which returned the case to the Court of Appeals for reassessment.

...Heather Osland remained unable to rest in her fight for truth.

The original decision was upheld and thus, despite being the catalyst for the way courts viewed provocation from the female perspective, Heather Osland remained unable to rest in her fight for truth.

Despite these setbacks, she continues to fight to this day, and will once more take her appeal to the High Court.

'TO HAVE AND TO HOLD'—
NO MATTER WHAT THE COST

James Ramage

By the time he reached his mid 40s, James Ramage enjoyed an enviable lifestyle.

His business career was rewarding, he had a beautiful wife, his two talented children attended prestigious private schools and he owned a luxurious home. This was, however, a facade, hiding an unhappy marriage, which, after years of unhappiness, finally imploded.

No longer able to be with the man she had married, 42-year-old Julie Ramage wanted out, asking James for a separation. Not long after, she left the family home, taking her daughter with her, to live in a separate dwelling. And, as fate would have it, in her 'new' life Julie embarked on a relationship with a man she felt a much deeper and more fruitful connection.

On 21 July 2003, six weeks had passed since she made the choice to leave her husband. Julie decided it was time to discuss personal problems with the sometimes violent man. Throughout that Melbourne winter, a tradesman had been completing renovations at the family home, and with this in mind, as she arrived back at her previous residence, Julie believed it was safe because someone else would be on the premises.

This decision proved fatal.

...hiding an unhappy marriage, which, after years of unhappiness, finally imploded.

...he knocked her to the ground and then strangled his wife with his bare hands.

Having sent the tradesman home early, Ramage was there alone to meet his wife. Their discussion turned sour when (according to Jame's Ramage's later testimony) Julie levelled at him that sex with him 'repulsed her'. This was apparently enough to push the man over the edge—he knocked her to the ground and then strangled his wife with his bare hands.

The deed done, Ramage dumped her corpse into the boot of his expensive Jaguar, which he drove to an outlying area of the city—ironically, the location where Julie had previously spent many happy hours riding horses. He buried the body in a shallow grave in the bushland terrain, made two bogus calls on Julie's mobile phone to help cover his tracks and returned home after choosing a marble bench top for his renovated kitchen.

Several hours later, he discussed his situation at length with close friend, criminal barrister Dyson Hore-Lacy SC, best known at the time as chair of the Fitzroy Football Club. Upon hearing this confession, Hore-Lacy called in another lawyer and later that evening James Ramage fronted at a nearby police station to turn himself in.

The case went to trial in October of that year, with the barrister for the defendant, Phil Dunn, QC, telling jurors and Justice Robert Osborn that Ramage did not deny killing his wife. The important question for the court to debate was whether Ramage had committed murder or manslaughter.

Dunn believed the prosecution could not prove the intent required for a murder conviction, saying there was no premeditation, and thus at issue was whether Ramage's actions took place under provocation, as defined by the law.

Julie Ramage

He supported his case by painting Julie Ramage as a hormone-fuelled, pleasure-seeking minx who cheated on her husband, exacerbating his fragile mental state. Calling on a psychologist Ramage had attended after his wife left him, Dunn successfully claimed the distraught husband suffered an adjustment disorder. When Julie Ramage told her husband she was going to leave him, and allegedly rejected his sexual prowess in comparison to her new lover, he had lost his self-control.

...a hormone-fuelled, pleasure-seeking minx who cheated on her husband...

While the defence counsel in court frequently mentioned Julie Ramage's two extra-marital affairs, several facts about her husband were kept from the court. His fidelity, for one, or rather lack of it, was not mentioned. Furthermore, an alleged 1991 assault when he reportedly broke his wife's nose and blackened her eyes after a head butting attack, was not communicated to the jury, despite James Leckie SC, relating to the court that Ramage was a driven, power-hungry tyrant who would do anything to get his wife back under his control.

Supporting this was testimony by the couple's seventeen-year-old daughter Samantha who recalled that her mother secretly organised leaving the family home because she worried her husband might get angry.

'That he'd do something to try and hurt her, like... kill the horses, or steal the horse float or control the money or something like that,' she said.

Dunn, however, had worked hard enough to ensure the murder rap could not stick, with the final verdict delivered as 'manslaughter by virtue of provocation', causing much public outcry. Justice Osborn sentenced Ramage to 11 years prison, but not without a parting swipe at the use of provocation his defence counsel had mounted.

'The killing was done with murderous intent and savage brutality'

'The killing was done with murderous intent and savage brutality,' Osborn proclaimed, 'and where, although the jury has accepted the reasonable possibility of provocation, it is apparent that such provocation was not objectively extreme.'

Julie Ramage's death, however, was not in vain.

Over 2500 letters sent to the Ramage family, passed onto the Victorian Attorney

General Robert Hulls and a Law Reform Commission established after the Ramage case, ensured a sweeping change, leading to the removal of the archaic provocation defence.

No longer would men be able to strike down their wives by the simple virtue of their marital connection.

JUSTIFIABLE HOMICIDE

Claire McDonald and her five children endured twenty years of sustained sadistic physical and verbal abuse and, as with Heather Osland, it came at the hands of the man who was supposed to love and protect them—Claire's own husband, Warren John MacDonald.

This constant harassment was noticed by the unhappy Victorian schoolteacher's closest friend, and to some extent her in-laws, who observed the 38-year-old woman and her children being continually humiliated in public. During the many years of her married hell, where she was often treated as nothing better than a slave, her husband often forced his wife to perform sexual acts she found disgusting, using anal sex as a form of punishment to further degrade her.

Eventually, in fear of her life, she devised a plan to escape his evil hold.

On 30 November 2004, Claire McDonald phoned the family home on Breakaway Mountain near Seymour to tell her son the Land Rover had stalled and that she was stranded. She meticulously described her location so that her husband would know where to come for help after he arrived home from work.

Had anyone seen her as she hid in wait for her husband to arrive, dressed in his cam-

...she was often treated as nothing better than a slave...

ouflage clothes and with a single shot rifle at the ready, they would have possibly raised the alarm at such a perplexing sight. When Warren MacDonald arrived and began tinkering with the engine of the Land Rover, she deliberately fired six single shots from 50 metres away, fatally shooting him.

Claire MacDonald

After firing the shots, she walked over to her dying husband, put her hands on him and, in her own words,

'…told him how much I hated him, and I hated him for making me do this'.

Prosecutor Ray Elston, SC said in opening the trial that Mrs MacDonald had lay in wait for 90 minutes before shooting her husband from a 'sniper's nest', executing him in a cold-blooded, calculated and determined way.

…executing him in a cold-blooded, calculated and determined way.

The prosecution also made much of the fact that there existed other rational options Claire McDonald should have taken, and that, even though his reprehensible behaviour may have been sadistic, the man should not have died for his sins.

Although plausible observations, a day and a half of deliberations by the jury returned a verdict of 'not-guilty', to either manslaughter or murder. What her defence team described as a 'stunning legal victory' was much more for Claire MacDonald, who could now live a life free of her cruel oppressor.

STRUCK DOWN

No one deserves to die at the hands of an angry lover.

When it is a 16-year-old, with so much life still ahead, the tragedy is multiplied exponentially.

Taryn Hunt was an attractive teen, high-spirited to the point of wilfulness. At the age of 14, she met a man who wowed her—26-year-old, Damian Sebo. They quickly became entangled, emotionally and physically, uncaring of her being underage and the legalities involved with such a sexual relationship.

...uncaring of her being underage and the legalities involved with such a sexual relationship.

Taryn's mother, Jenny Tierney, knew her daughter well enough to have little doubt that expressing any disapproval of the age difference would have little bearing on her daughter's decision to be in the relationship. When Taryn indicated she wanted to move in with Sebo, Jenny did the one thing she hoped would at least keep her daughter within the general sphere of her authority—she allowed Sebo to move into their Pacific Pines home, north-east of Surfers Paradise.

And, truth be known, Jenny had seen Sebo be something of a positive influence in her daughter's life.

There was another side, however—a side that should have rung alarm bells in Tierney's mind. Sebo was fiercely possessive. He would demand Taryn accompany him to watch him referee basketball, his other true love. A coach at one of the games, who observed the couple said,

'She was there, sitting straight up, like a cattle dog waiting outside a shop for its owner. She watched him and he would look over constantly. Her eyes never left him. She never moved. She just sat there. It was odd to me, like she was hypnotised.'

Unbeknownst to Sebo, Taryn was growing out of the relationship, and they eventually split. Strangely, Sebo remained living with her and her mother, and his obsessive love for her remained alive.

At about 1.30am on 7 September 2005, the pair was driving home after they had been out drinking at Conrad Jupiters Casino, celebrating Taryn leaving school. An argument broke out when Taryn told Sebo she wanted to see other men, asking him to drop her at another man's house that very night. Brazenly, she went on to taunt Sebo with details of sexual exploits with other men, boasting how easy it was for her to cheat on him behind his back.

...boasting how easy it was for her to cheat on him behind his back.

Taryn should have known that this kind of revelation was fuel to the fire for her possessive ex-boyfriend, but whether the alcohol had her not thinking straight or she underestimated what his reaction might be, we will never know.

Outraged, Sebo pulled over near the southbound Coomera exit on the Pacific Motorway. Grabbing the steering lock, he savagely struck her head with it, not once but several times. Under his fierce blows, she sustained multiple fractures to her head, eye socket and wrist.

Grabbing the steering lock, he savagely struck her head with it...

Realising what he had done, Sebo rushed Hunt to the Gold Coast Hospital, by which time she was in a coma. During her last two days alive, she apparently gripped her mother's hand, a sign that she still somehow clung to life within the shattered form, but never spoke.

Two days later, medical staff turned Taryn's life support off when doctors declared her brain dead.

Initially, at a police interview, Sebo told officers he had in fact left Hunt on the side of the road after their argument, then returned late to find her beaten up, laying in a garden bed. However, after two hours of questioning, and upon the presentation of contradictory witness accounts, Sebo broke down, confessing.

'You got me, I did it. I don't know why it happened.'

When the case finally came to trial in the middle of 2007, Sebo, charged with murder, pleaded not guilty, instead admitting to the lesser offence of manslaughter. His defence attorney argued that there was no intent in the death of Hunt on Sebo's behalf and that Sebo was provoked by the young woman.

The trial lasted six days and, after deliberating for over two days, the jury returned a not guilty verdict to the murder charge, accepting Sebo's defence that Taryn's taunting had provoked the deadly attack.

He was jailed for 10 years for manslaughter.

Family and friends of Hunt, and members of the public, felt dismay and outrage at the verdict and sentence, and, as with the Ramage case in Victoria, the decision sparked calls for an overhaul of the provocation defence.

In November 2007, the Attorney General, Kerry Shine argued Damian Karl Sebo's 10-year jail sentence should be increased to 12 to 14 years on the grounds that the original sentence was manifestly inadequate.

The courts did not agree.

Ross Martin SC, for the Attorney General, presented to the Court of Appeals that, even allowing for mitigating circumstances such as remorse and a guilty plea to manslaughter, Sebo's sentence was insufficient.

However, Tony Moynihan SC for Sebo argued that of the 15 previous cases presented

...accepting Sebo's defence that Taryn's taunting had provoked the deadly attack.

...13 supported a sentence of nine to ten years...

to the court of a similar nature, 13 supported a sentence of nine to ten years and that the eight years Sebo would be forced to serve was in no way a light sentence.

The court unanimously dismissed the appeal.

A year later, The Queensland Law Reform Commission recommended provocation be excluded as a defence in cases where 'a victim's words or their decision to end a relationship was the justification for killing them, except in extreme and exceptional circumstances.'

At the time of print, the Commission's recommendations about the defence of provocation had not yet been implemented. However, a Bill has recently been introduced to provide a defence for battered persons.

Damian Sebo and Taryn Hunt

A WILD WOMAN

Anthony Sherna

Sometimes it takes the smallest things to tip someone over the edge.

For 42-year-old Anthony Sherna, it was something as simple as unkindness to his Russell-Maltese cross, Hubble, that pushed him too far.

Sherna did not have the happiest of childhoods.

The Chernishoff (Sherna's name before he was forced to change it) family were well acquainted with domestic violence. Sherna's vision was damaged in utero when his alcoholic father punched his mother in the stomach, and she was continually victimised by her husband until she divorced him when Sherna was a toddler. Sherna grew up with tales of his father's rages, including an episode when a noose was hung around the neck of an older brother.

...a noose was hung around the neck of an older brother.

Thus, it might come as no surprise that when a relationship of his own came along at the age of 23, Sherna might unwittingly fall into a less than healthy situation.

Almost from the moment he met Susan Wild, ten years his senior, Sherna completely lost his autonomy—he was smitten with the woman with who his relationship would eventually come to more resemble some twisted

Susanne Wild

Wild picked Sherna's clothes, rationed his money and cigarettes...

maternal bond than that of lovers.

Wild picked Sherna's clothes, rationed his money and cigarettes (despite him being the breadwinner), dictated what they watched on television and made him sleep on a camp bed in a spare room. Referring to him as a 'low-life', she constantly accused him of having affairs. She refused him sex, taking up with a former lover at one point and telling Sherna to 'grow some balls'. Workmates reported she sometimes called him at work as many as 12 times a day, severely limiting his chances of promotion, and even made him use public toilets when he was out of the house rather than the one at home.

Sherna endured this emotional abuse as a 'battered spouse' for 18 years. However, it would finally end on the evening of 1 February 2008.

That night, after one of their regular arguments, Sherna went to the laundry of their Tarneit home in the westerns suburbs of Melbourne to complete his nightly ritual of rocking his dog Hubble to sleep.

When an inebriated Wild came in to continue the argument as Sherna held his small dog, quivering for fear in his arms, he decided he had had enough. Following Wild back into the kitchen, he grabbed the cord from his dressing gown and, even as she tried to engage with him in their argument once more, wrapped it around her throat, strangling her.

The deed done, Sherna left the house to go drinking, then visited a brothel in the early hours of 2 February before returning to the house.

Over the next few days, as Wild's body began to decompose, Sherna disposed of the putrefying corpse by digging a one-metre deep hole in the backyard. It was not until over a week after her death that police finally investigated, tipped off by one of Sherna's brothers.

He confessed without hesitation, pleading not guilty to murder under the 'defensive homicide' act, introduced in 2005, to account for killings occurring as a result of sustained domestic violence and abuse, and was remanded to stand trial in the Supreme Court.

Defence lawyer, Jane Dixon SC, argued Sherna had been in a grossly dysfunctional relationship, controlled and dominated by his partner to a pathological extent, enduring a horrific relationship in which he suffered some form or another of daily abuse.

Given the demise of the defence of provocation, there was no way Sherna could be excused the death of Wild, and in October 2009, a jury found him not guilty of murder but rather of the alternative charge of manslaughter.

...Sherna disposed of the putrefying corpse by digging a one-metre deep hole in the backyard.

In sentencing, Justice David Beach said,

'I accept that the deceased was both controlling and domineering of you, and that from time to time this involved significant episodes of unpleasantness.'

Justice Beach went on to say that nothing would justify or excuse Sherna killing his partner...

However, Justice Beach went on to say that nothing would justify or excuse Sherna killing his partner, sentencing him to 14 years, with a minimum term of ten years.

So, although he had released himself from an emotional prison, the means by which he achieved this were outside of the law, and served only to land him in a more concrete penitentiary.

Maybe, when he is released sometimes in his fifties, he will finally have his first real taste of freedom since taking up with Wild all those years ago.

EVIL STEPFATHER

Shae Ballinger, a Mooroopna girl, had her life shattered, barely into her teens at the age of 14.

Allegedly, the four-year cycle of sexual abuse began at this point when she virtually became her stepfather's sex slave. Sexual penetration and oral sex was demanded of her as often as twice a day. Any refusal was greeted with threats to kill her. The trapped teenager had no doubt that, in her own words, 'he would have stabbed me straight in the heart' if she divulged details about their abusive relationship to her mother or local police.

Russel Frik, a 34-year-old truck driver and diesel mechanic, lived with his 39-year-old de facto wife, their three young sons and Shae in a rundown brick house in the Victorian country town of Mooroopna. At the back of the property was a large tin shed where the de facto stepfather sexually abused the defenceless teenager while her mother was working nightshift. Police later recovered around 10 000 explicit photographs Frik took during these forced sexual encounters.

On 13 March 2008, the predatory beast demanded oral sex from Shae in the shed just an hour after sex was forced on her in the house. He pointed a loaded gun at her when

Police later recovered around 10 000 explicit photographs Frik took...

she refused, so she complied. However, when the weapon was left against the wall, the desperate young woman seized her opportunity for revenge, grabbing it and shooting him in the back of the head.

She fled the house after throwing a sheet over the dead body.

...Shae unsuccessfully attempted to burn the corpse...

The next night, Shae unsuccessfully attempted to burn the corpse, and when this failed, dismembered the body with a saw. She took most parts of his severed body to the nearby Cemetery Bend State Forest where she stuffed his arms and legs down two bush toilets and threw his head into nearby bushes.

Later, she buried the torso in the vegetable garden at their home.

The remains lay undiscovered for another month, during which time the 18- year-old killer sent text messages from the deceased man's mobile phone to convince the family the missing man was still alive. However, by April, suspicious police apprehended the young woman and before long recovered the dismembered corpse.

The girl's mother later stated she had questioned her de facto partner on at least four occasions about the true nature of his relationship with her daughter. Detectives claimed that some teachers at the local secondary school ignored their duty of care with regard to the young woman's welfare. During her time in Years 8, 9 and 10, three concerned students reportedly voiced their concerns about bruises, which periodically appeared on their classmate's upper arms and shoulders. Since 2007, it had become mandatory for all teachers to pass on such reports to the Department of Human Services. If the local teachers had addressed this responsibility at an early stage, police maintained the alleged abuse would have been investigated and that the homicide may never have taken place.

Shae Ballinger was charged with murder, appearing before the Shepparton Magistrates' Court. Peter Chadwick, her defence, argued that the motive for her actions was simple... so that 'she wouldn't have to do it again'. Under cross-examination, Victoria Police homicide squad Detective Senior Constable Barry Gray said that of the many images seized, while some were of the pair engaged in sexual activity, 'by far the large majority were of just the accused'. He agreed that among the images was one of the accused tied to a chair with cable ties and towels, and concluded that given the images dated from January 2004 until February 2008, constituted child pornography.

Chadwick also argued that,

'He (Frik) had used the images to blackmail her into submission. Asked by police

'He (Frik) had used the images to blackmail her into submission...

161

...she probably would have killed herself because she could not keep living the way she was.'

what she thought would have happened if she hadn't killed him, she said she probably would have killed herself because she could not keep living the way she was.'

Crown prosecutor Mark Gamble counter-argued, believing that Ballinger's dismembering of the body and attempts to cover up the murder could be construed as something other than self-defence.

The eighteen-year-old was remanded to appear before the Supreme Court on a charge of murder in March 2009. Victoria's Director of Public Prosecution, Jeremy Rapke, QC, withdrew the murder charge during the Supreme Court hearing, stating such came after 'careful consideration' of the strength of the evidence. He believed there was 'no reasonable prospect' a jury could convict the girl.

Justice Philip Cummins proclaimed the decision was 'responsible and necessary', and on 27 March, Shae Ballinger left the court with her mother by her side, both weeping tears of joy at being freed from both the charges laid and the beast who had for so long held her in his thrall.

SECTION FOUR:

FAMILY AFFAIRS

Murder is unique in that it abolishes the party it injures,
So that society has to take the place of the victim
And on his behalf demand atonement or grant forgiveness;
It is the one crime in which society has a direct interest.

W. H. Auden

The pressures of family and, especially child rearing, can sometimes be too great for individuals to bear, leading them to commit crimes against those they are supposed to nurture and protect.

These 'family affairs' have an essence about them which, although may not make them true crimes of passion, do at least align the incidents with them in certain ways. They are always the product of intense emotions—jealousy or rage, depression or despair, desperation or destitution—committed in a moment where this emotion overwhelms and pushes individuals to action with the worst kind of outcome.

Sadly, they also often involve children, where, in the most tragic case, love has curdled into dark thoughts, leading to murderous intent.

CHAPTER 7

FAMILY TIES

ALL THAT GLITTERS

Gloria Krope was crowned Miss Australia in 1977 and, to all observers, the world was her oyster.

However, the glamorous woman's public life was in sharp contrast to the simmering tensions that existed in Gloria Krope's family home.

Frederick Krope and his wife Josephine raised their three children, Gloria, Rosemary and William, in the Melbourne suburb of Glenroy after emigrating from Yugoslavia in 1951. Krope worked mainly as a fitter and turner in his adopted country, but the quick-tempered, unpredictable man never provided the security his family needed.

He was both a gambling addict and sadistic bully who regularly abused his wife and family, whose violent behaviour was so intense that Rosemary suffered a nervous breakdown, consequently receiving psychiatric treatment.

Gloria herself, in fear of her own life, had moved

from the family residence in 1972 to escape the tyranny.

In the week before Christmas 1977, Krope went too far.

...bought a rifle as a means of protecting his family should their father ever go too far.

After calling his wife a slut and refusing money to finance the family Christmas celebrations, Krope's son fought back against years of tyranny. The distraught young man had bought a rifle as a means of protecting his family should their father ever go too far. On the evening of 21 December, Krope disappeared into the garage and, fearing his father had gone there to get the rifle her kept, William armed himself.

As Frederick Krope stormed into the house to confront his family, a hail of bullets greeted him (27 spent cartridges were later found at the crime scene.)

Soon after, police were summoned to the Krope's Simms Crescent residence where they discovered the body of Frederick Krope, lying in a pool of blood. They charged William Krope with his father's murder and later went on to implicate his mother.

At their subsequent trial, William Krope provided a graphic account of what life was like in the dysfunctional family home.

'No-one could believe what we've been through and what sort of a man he was...Fear was with us all the time...I was terrified of him for as long as I could remember…I believe he was truly mad…'

And, indeed, things were so bad in the Krope household that William himself had attempted suicide in September 1977.

William Krope's trial defence barrister was Frank Galbally, in a case that would prove to be his making professionally. A persuasive advocate, he cleverly turned public opinion against the murder victim after showing jury members the peephole Fredrick Krope made in his bathroom wall so he could watch his daughters showering.

Such deviant behaviour increased abhorrence towards the dead man.

After deliberating for seven hours, the jury found neither William nor his mother guilty of Frederick Krope's murder, a decision generally hailed as just and fair by the public.

…the peephole Fredrick Krope made in his bathroom wall so he could watch his daughters showering.

William Krope with his mother, Josephine

THE ULTIMATE REVENGE

Brian Altham was a bitter man.

The former Australian Army Major had endured 12 months of loneliness and despair following the collapse of his ten-year marriage. Most of all, he resented having limited access to his two daughters.

In December 1978, the estranged husband waited in a Perth suburb for his wife, Elizabeth, to return home from a shopping trip. When the unsuspecting woman arrived, Altham struck her on the back of the head with a sand-filled sock, before gagging, binding and throwing her into the boot of his car.

He drove to his flat where six-year-old Samantha and four-year-old Cherand were staying with him on an access visit. Collecting his two children, Altham conveyed his family to a bush location.

Once there, he tied his wife to a tree and drove off again with their two daughters. Twenty minutes later, Brian returned and, after untying Elizabeth, forced her into a Vietnamese-style bunker, approximately three metres long, and a metre deep and wide, supported by poles and a sheet of iron.

Sealing the entrance with bricks, Altham offered Elizabeth the option of suicide by slashing her wrists, which she refused. He secured

...struck her on the back of the head with a sand-filled sock...

her tightly and, as he left her to die from suffocation, consumed copious amounts of sleeping tablets in an attempt to end his own life.

Elizabeth eventually managed to free herself.

Seeing her unconscious ex-husband, she tied his wrists tightly together and removed the bricks from the bunker entrance, escaping to a nearby road. Eventually, the distressed woman managed to flag down a passing motorist who drove her to nearby Brentwood police station.

After Elizabeth described her dangerous ordeal, a massive police hunt began. They soon found the unconscious Brian Altham in the bunker and rushed him to hospital, where doctors resuscitated him. Further investigations uncovered similar bunkers nearby with Brian even placing a fake bomb outside one of them as a decoy.

The girls remained missing.

Rescuers intensified their efforts to find them and, within two days, the outcome everyone feared became a grim reality when two bodies were found in a bush grave about four kilometres from the bunker area. Both had perished from severe head injuries, most likely from the blows of a hammer.

...two bodies were found in a bush grave...

Before court proceedings even began, the Vietnam veteran attempted to hang himself in his prison cell, but survived. At his subsequent

...Altham pleaded not guilty to two charges of murder on the grounds of insanity...

trial, Brian Altham pleaded not guilty to two charges of murder on the grounds of insanity, but the court ignored his plea for clemency.

Altham was found guilty as charged, and sentenced to death, a decision later commuted to life imprisonment.

VICTIMS OF A TORTURED MOTHER

Kathleen Folbigg

When parents lose a child to Sudden Infant Death Syndrome (SIDS), or 'cot death', it is a tragic misfortune.

Sometimes, however, tragedy seems to run in the family, in one shape or another, and there is little that can be done to prevent the tragic cycle of loss perpetuating itself.

In the case of Kathleen Folbigg, the multiple cases of 'bad luck' proved to be more about 'bad' than 'luck'.

A modern-day Medea was in the making.

Kathleen's early life was traumatic. On a balmy evening just before Christmas in 1968, her father stabbed her mother 24 times in a frenzy of rage because he believed she was negligent in her care of their daughter. In the aftermath of this tragedy, she was placed in foster care at the age of three.

...her father stabbed her mother 24 times in a frenzy of rage...

Fostered out, while growing up Kathleen clashed at times with her foster mother, just as any teen does, but overall was raised in a predictable and stable home. She was 18 before she learned of the violent murder of her birth mother.

From that time onwards, the grim aspect of her family history remained a constant torment.

At the age of 20, she married local steel worker, Craig Folbigg, and the couple established a home in the Newcastle suburb of Mayfield. Within a year, Kathleen became pregnant with Caleb, but he died 19 days after his birth on 20 February 1989, presumably of SIDS. Family members were thus overjoyed when Kathleen fell pregnant once more and gave birth to Patrick on 1 June 1990.

By October, Patrick was experiencing breathing problems and eventually died on 13 February 1991. On this occasion, the official cause of death was listed as acute asphyxiation, believed to have resulted from an epileptic fit.

In October 1992, the Folbigg's welcomed their first daughter Sarah into the world, but once again tragedy stalked the Folbiggs when she too perished before reaching her first birthday. Doctors diagnosed SIDS as responsible for the infant's sudden demise.

The Folbiggs relocated to Singleton in 1997, and not long after their fourth child Laura was born.

The breathing and sleep patterns of the new baby were monitored carefully, but at the age of 19 months, she developed a cold. Local emergency services were contacted when the child experienced breathing difficulties and when paramedics arrived at the Folbigg residence they found Kathleen frantically

Local emergency services were contacted when the child experienced breathing difficulties...

applying CPR to Laura.

Unfortunately, the best efforts of all proved unsuccessful, and the small girl died.

Doctors considered this baby too old to have died from SIDS and the term 'undetermined' was used to describe the official cause of the fourth fatality. However, suspicions were now aroused, sparking a police investigation to determine the causes of the multiple deaths.

Craig Folbigg initially remained convinced that Kathleen was innocent of any wrongdoing, arguing his wife loved having children—she loved the feeling of a baby moving inside her and was pleased when her children grew fat and apparently healthy. She had also responded to their deaths with 'blood-curdling screams', so deep was her agony.

Then, to his horror, Craig unexpectedly came across one of his wife's diaries, at which time it became obvious that she had taken each of their lives.

'With Sarah,' one entry read, 'all I wanted her to do was shut up. And one day she did.'

Another extract revealed Kathleen Folbigg's tormented state of mind.

'(I) would like all my mistakes and terrible thinking to be corrected and mean something, though obviously I'm my father's daughter.'

Many other entries were just as chilling.

Police arrested Kathleen Folbigg shortly

She had also responded to their deaths with 'blood-curdling screams'...

...the jury found her guilty of all four murders, sentencing her to 40 years in custody...

after the diary was handed to them. At her trial, the jury found her guilty of all four murders, sentencing her to 40 years in custody, with a non-parole period of 30 years. This term was later reduced, meaning Folbigg could be free in 2029.

In 2009, her lawyer made an unsuccessful attempt to force a retrial due to a miscarriage of justice. Before the Court of Criminal Appeals, he argued that in Folbigg's first trial the actions of several jurors in obtaining information about Folbigg's father were prejudicial to her receiving a fair trial.

The Court of Criminal Appeal was unanimous in quashing this appeal.

Kathleen Folbigg (who still stridently maintains her innocence) is serving her sentence at Mulwala Women's Prison, where she is often isolated from other inmates because of fears for her life. Her husband has re-married, maintaining no contact with her.

Criminal psychologists have exhaustively investigated Kathleen's case history. Melbourne psychiatrist, Anne Buist, believes Folbigg has a narcissistic personality. The lack of love in her early childhood produced an ego that labelled her own children as being her possessions, with her resenting them developing their own distinct personalities. The infants' nurturing-needs conflicted with the mother's personal emotional needs and the outcomes that flowed from this problem proved to be horrific. When attention moved away from the needs of Kathleen Folbigg to a newly born baby, this insecure mother felt as abandoned as she had been in her own childhood.

Her sense of insecurity was also clearly prevalent in other areas of her life.

During her marriage, she was often jealous of her husband's supposed attentions to other women and harboured long-term grudges over trivial issues. She also wrote often in her diary that she felt hurt by her husband's taunts about her weight and looks, something she was determined to sort out so that she would not lose him. Overall, it would seem Kathleen's fractured personality produced a woman who felt compelled to kill her own children.

...Kathleen's fractured personality produced a woman who felt compelled to kill her own children.

Perhaps the most telling of all her diary entries was one she wrote when pregnant with Laura.

'Thirty years. The first five I don't really remember, the rest, I choose not to remember. The last 10-11 have been filled with trauma, tragedy, happiness and mixed emotions of all designs. If it wasn't for my baby coming soon, I'd sit and wonder again what I was put on this earth for. What contribution have I made to anyone's life?'

Chilling words, written by a woman who

clearly had no love for herself and was thus, as a consequence, unable to truly love the children she bore.

IN FOLBIGG'S SHADOW?

The deaths of Carol Matthey's children began on 8 December 1998.

Carol Matthey

Her first child, seven-month-old Jacob was discovered dead by Matthey in his cot. SIDS was the official cause of death on the death certificate.

Eleven months later, Matthey's nine-week-old daughter Chloe also succumbed to SIDS and then, in July 2002, Joshua Matthey stopped breathing when he was lying in his pram in a shopping centre car park.

His cause of death was listed as klebsiella septicaemia.

Just over two years later, Carol Matthey called for an ambulance when her fourth child, three-year-old Shania, stopped breathing. Shania had fallen from a coffee table the day prior and the next morning after Carol showered she grew concerned Shania had not yet arisen.

Going to her room, she discovered her daughter wasn't breathing and attempted CPR. Having little success, she called in paramedics. They arrived and tried further resuscitation, but to no avail.

...she discovered her daughter wasn't breathing and attempted CPR.

The coroner noted the cause of death as 'unascertained' which, as with the earlier Folbigg case this situation was worryingly mim-

...uncover the causes of the multiple infant deaths in the Matthey family.

icking, led police to launch an exhaustive investigation to uncover the causes of the multiple infant deaths in the Matthey family.

Police interviewed over 160 witnesses during the next three years as evidence was painstakingly gathered. Melbourne Magistrate Duncan Reynolds decided there was enough evidence for Matthey to appear in the Supreme Court, which she did on 4 July 2006, to face four charges of murder.

However, the case never went to trial when Paul Coghlan QC, the Victorian Director of Public Prosecutions (DPP), declared there to be not enough evidence for Matthey to be charged.

This decision, clearly a setback for the prosecution case, in legal terms did not represent an acquittal per se, and if new evidence surfaces, the opportunity exists for the case to be reopened.

Why did Coghlan do this?

Confusing opinions from established experts made a clear-cut decision difficult for the DPP.

An American paediatric forensic expert, Dr. Janice Ophoven, in possession of an enviable international reputation on the causes of infant deaths, firmly supported the prosecution case. She had previously played a significant role in the prosecution's submissions when Kathleen Folbigg was convicted, and had come to the conclusion in the Matthey case with a 'reasonable degree of medical certainty' that Jacob, Shania and Joshua were victims of intentional suffocation.

Further evidence came from a South Australian paediatrician, Dr Susan Beal, who backed Ophoven's claims. She argued the lack of risk factors for SIDS in some of the children, the troubled Matthey marriage and the fact that the children had experienced 'ALTEs' ('apparent life-threatening episodes') in which they stopped breathing or were found unconscious. Dr Beal argued that,

'...these ALTEs are not a predictor for SIDS, they're a predictor for (homicide).'

In contrast, Stephen Cordner, the Director of the Victorian Institute of Forensic Medicine, found no evidence of foul play in any of the deaths.

'I believe her statement is flawed in its assumptions, reasoning and conclusions,' he said in his statement. 'Dr Ophoven's homicide hypothesis, when shorn of its trappings, rests on a relatively small number of shaky foundations.'

The DPP's decision was strongly supported by Matthey's defence team.

At the previous March 2006 committal hearing, they argued there was no physical

... Jacob, Shania and Joshua were victims of intentional suffocation.

evidence of harm to any of the deceased children. All deaths, they maintained, were probably due to a shared, at present unidentified, genealogical defect.

Justice Coldrey ruled out most of the evidence of Beal and Ophoven, which meant the Crown case relied on other evidence, such as Mrs Matthey's relationship with her husband and children. He also found there was no discernible link between the timing of marital crises and the ALTEs or the deaths, and while there was some evidence of poor mothering, there was enough indication that Matthey truly grieved for the deaths of her children.

...there was some evidence of poor mothering...

Speaking after the case, Mrs Matthey's lawyer, Paul Lacava, SC, proclaimed there to be no real winners in the case.

'Mrs Matthey and her husband have lost their children and their sadness is profound and ongoing. The only winner is the justice system itself.'

A HUSBAND SCORNED

In August 2005, Greg King and Robert Farquharson met outside a fish & chip shop in Winchelsea, Victoria.

Life had turned sour for King's old friend.

Robert Farquharson

Farquharson was receiving medical care for depression following the break-up of his marriage, and his former wife had become a financial burden. She also had custody of their three children and a new man had come into her life.

According to King, the rejected and angry husband allegedly vowed to 'take away the things that mean the most to her', adding he had formulated a plan that would involve the three children on some special day so that their mother would always suffer on that particular anniversary.

On Father's Day, two months later, when an access visit with his three sons was ending, Robert Farquharson's was driving his three boys back to their mother's when somehow his car left the road in the early evening and sank beneath the waters of a dam. The father managed to escape from the vehicle, but ten-year-old Jai, seven year-old Tyler and two-year-old Bailey all drowned.

Later, Farquharson claimed he had tempo-

...the rejected and angry husband allegedly vowed to 'take away the things that mean the most to her'...

rarily blacked out at the wheel of the car after suffering a severe coughing fit that caused his out of control vehicle to veer off the road and into the dam. He then reportedly dived into the water in an unsuccessful effort to rescue his sons.

However, police officers who arrived at the fatal scene became sceptical about Farquharson's explanations. They noticed that the tyre marks between the fence and the water showed no evidence of the car having veered suddenly off the road. It also seemed strange that Farquharson refused all offers of help from bystanders and that he twice ignored opportunities to contact emergency services. He also stood on the dam bank and watched while his wife's new partner repeatedly dived under the water, desperate to locate the boys.

...person- ally inform her about the heartbreak- ing triple fatalities.

Farquharson did, however, clamber back onto the highway, where he persuaded a parked motorist to drive him eight kilometres to his wife's home so that he could personally inform her about the heartbreaking triple fatalities.

Early the next day, police divers discovered the bodies of the children and the car was dragged from the dam. They discovered that both the older boys had managed to free themselves from their seat belts while the car was sinking, but had drowned attempting to free Bailey from his harness. It also emerged that that the car's lights had been turned off before the car sank below beneath the dam and that the mechanical condition of the vehicle was sound.

Two days after the fatalities occurred, after questioning him in his home, police charged Robert Farquharson with three counts of murder. At his subsequent trial, it was emphasised that the accused had no previous history of coughing attacks and his reported conversation with Gary King was also damaging to his defence's case. Handing down his sentence, Justice Philip Cummins talked about the need for the law to protect vulnerable children.

'If the law fails there, the law fails,' Justice Cummins said.

Then he turned to Farquharson with a damning statement.

'You wiped out your entire family in one act. Only the two parents remained: you, because you had always intended to save yourself; and their mother, because you intended her to live a life of suffering.'

He went on to sentence Farquharson to a life imprisonment for each life taken, without parole.

Initially, his ex-wife, Cindy Gambino, supported her ex-husband's claims of innocence.

'He would not harm a hair of their heads,' she declared. 'It was an accident...I don't

'You wiped out your entire family in one act.'

...she sought unspecified damages for suffering nervous shock, anxiety, depression and post-traumatic stress...

believe that it was murder...'

However, Gambino abandoned her support for him in a civil action in the Supreme Court in May 2009, where she sought unspecified damages for suffering nervous shock, anxiety, depression and post-traumatic stress in the aftermath of the triple murders. On 15 May, Justice Phillip Cummins upheld her compensation claim, ordering Robert Farquharson to pay $225 000 in damages. Unfortunately for the claimant, she may receive far less than this amount as Farquharson maintains he only has $66 000 in assets.

In June 2009, Farquharson's defence team appealed his decision in the Supreme Court on the grounds of the prosecution's key witness, King, being unreliable and tainted. The court rejected the appeal.

However, in a massive turnaround, on 17 December 2009, Judges Marilyn Warren, Geoffrey Nettle and Robert Redlich accepted an appeal by Farquharson's defence team against the guilty verdict, quashing his conviction, and setting aside his sentence.

This decision was made on because they believed that the prosecution had 'wrongly failed to disclose' to Mr Farquharson's defence team during the trial that King had criminal charges pending against him. Warren, Nettle and Redlich also found that Justice Cummins did not properly instruct the jury as to how much weight it should give to Mr King's evidence and the taped conversations between himself and Mr Farquharson. He also failed in his directions regarding the prosecution's argument that Mr Farquharson's urging of his friend not tell police about their conversation was evidence of his guilty conscience.

Farquharson immediately applied for bail and will stand for retrial in 2010.

A LITTLE ANGEL FALLS

Arthur Freeman

On a warm morning in the middle of a warm Melbourne summer, peak-hour motorists taking the West Gate Bridge from Melbourne's western suburbs into the city saw a man standing by his white Land Cruiser at the bridge's highest point.

Some slowed to see what he was up to, as the West Gate is well known for 'jumpers'—attempted suicides.

It was not, however, his own death this man was contemplating, and these curious motorists were about to become the unwitting witnesses to the horrifying death of a little girl just a few days shy of her fifth birthday.

After returning from living in England in 2007, despite being unable to find employment as a computer programmer, Arthur Freeman reportedly enjoyed life as a stay-at-home father, caring for his three children, Benjamin, Darcey and Jonathon.

His wife, Peta, however, found it difficult dealing with his lack of work and mood swings for so long. Having had enough, she left him in March 2008, taking the children with her.

She warned her doctor that Freeman suffered incredible mood swings and believed him capable of harming her children, possibly even of killing them. She sensed that such would be

...believed him capable of harming her children, possibly even of killing them.

186

partially motivated by revenge against her for leaving him.

While Freeman was in the UK, Peta went to the courts to apply for full custody of the children, and was successful in late January 2009.

Speaking to him later, she thought he seemed happy with the decision of shared custody.

Little did she know, her actions would be part of the catalyst to push him into a place of absolute despair…a place where only tragedy could follow.

On the night of 28 January 2009, Freeman took his three children to his parent's beach house to escape the intolerably hot Melbourne summer's night, allegedly promising to take five-year-old Darcey and Benjamin to school the next morning.

It was to be Darcey's first day of school.

Clearly, the stress and pain of the custody battle had taken its toll on the man, and it must have shown, because the next morning Freeman's father, Peter, tried to stop him leaving to drive the children back to Melbourne, something his son would not hear of.

Some tightly coiled morass of sadness and anger and maybe a dash of madness must have snapped inside Arthur Freeman as he crossed the West Gate. Stopping his vehicle, he appar-

…Freeman's father, Peter, tried to stop him leaving to drive the children back to Melbourne…

...flung her over the side, where she hurtled the 58 metres into the murky waters below.

ently dragged what appeared to be a listless Darcey from the car, lifting her into his arms, where she allegedly hung rag-doll-limp.

Crossing to the edge of the bridge, with no sign of protest from his daughter, he flung her over the side, where she hurtled the 58 metres into the murky waters below.

Freeman returned to his car and drove off as motorists frantically called police.

By the time the water police arrived, a police hunt had begun for the white Land Cruiser. Darcey's body was retrieved from the water and, remarkably, she was alive, albeit in a critical condition with internal injuries.

At 10.30am, a man with two young boys wandered into the Commonwealth Law Courts in the city, which house the Family Law Courts. He seemed agitated and distressed, crying uncontrollably, and staff, trained in recognising such, immediately called for the police.

Even though his sons clung desperately to him, he approached security guards, begging them to take them from him. Unable to talk properly, it would be Benjamin who would tell the guards his name.

Police arrived not long after, handcuffing and arresting the man. Taken into custody, it is believed Freeman continued crying and was constantly shaking, and, despite still being unable to utter a word, police charged him with murder.

For Darcey had died at 1.30pm, her distraught mother by her side.

Freeman was remanded in custody for his committal hearing in October 2009, at which time a trial date was fixed for 7 April 2010. It is already believed that the mental impairment defence will be used by Freeman's legal team.

Freeman was remanded in custody for his committal hearing in October 2009...

Darcey Freeman

SECTION FIVE

RANDOM CRIMES
OF PASSION

Short of homicide, [rape] is the ultimate violation of self

Byron R. White

A sideways step from the general notion of crimes of passion are situations where individuals play out their fantasies or are unable to contain their so-called 'passion', usually in the form of lust or violence against hapless victims.

While not traditional crimes of passion due to their random nature, the element of sexual gratification and abuse that often comes with them, and the superficial passion associated, meaning these crimes may loosely be construed in the same vein.

Such random acts are often fuelled by drugs and alcohol—triggers which set off latent (or not so latent) psychotic tendencies, lived out as lust, the desire to inflict pain and suffering, and worst of all to take a life, by some of society's most wicked and damaged predators.

CHAPTER 8

SINGLE GUARDIANS
OF DEATH

BEAUTY STALKED BY EVIL

Neighbours noted how happy and attractive young couple Dorothy Denzel and Frank Wilkinson appeared before they zipped away in Frank's impressive red car for a picnic outing in Sydney on 6 April 1932.

By the end of the day, when the pair failed to return to their homes, admiration had turned to anxiety. Fears grew more pronounced after witnesses reported that a man, not matching Frank's description, was spotted driving the red car.

And in the back seat, there appeared to be a large, covered object.

Soon after, on 11 April 1932, Frank Wilkinson's body was discovered in a shallow grave on a bush track, his face badly bashed and the back of his head blown away by what appeared to be a shotgun blast fired at close range.

Four days later, a second grim discovery was unearthed.

...her hands tied behind her back with strips of rug, and a pullover was wrapped around her body...

Onlookers gathered as police exhumed the body of Dorothy Denzel. Closer examination revealed she had been shot at close range. She was naked, her hands tied behind her back with strips of rug, and a pullover was wrapped around her body—her dress was caught up around her neck.

A coroner later found she had been raped.

Police investigations quickly produced vital evidence. After Frank Wilkinson's car was located in a rented garage, witnesses revealed that a man with a bandaged hand had been seen driving the car near the time of the murder. Another important breakthrough followed when a mask cut from hessian was found in the garage.

Before long, well-known criminal William Moxley (aka William Fletcher) emerged as a prime suspect. He had been seen in the area with what appeared to be an injured hand, and when his Burwood home was raided, a hessian bag was discovered with a small face-sized section cut from it.

A massive manhunt began, centring largely on the suburb of Bankstown. Moxley brazenly rode a stolen bicycle through a police cordon in an effort to escape, but was cornered on the other side of the city. After a brief struggle, he was arrested and charged with two counts of murder.

In court, the awful story slowly unravelled.

The couple had been confronted by Moxley, who demanded money from them. When a mere seven shillings was all that was forthcoming, Moxley had tied up Wilkinson and taken the couple to an abandoned house, where he and Wilkinson had fought.

Finally, he had relocated to quiet bushland where he could silence them.

Moxley pleaded insanity and his lawyers were quick to point out that most of the evidence was circumstantial. Despite this, and Moxley's original confession in which there was no indication of premeditation, after the closing summations the jury returned three hours later with a guilty verdict. The judge declared Moxley's crimes as 'one of the foulest ever known in New South Wales', going on quickly to pass the death penalty.

On 18 August 1932, he became the first man to be hanged in NSW in nearly a decade.

The judge declared Moxley's crimes as 'one of the foulest ever known in New South Wales...

THE VOICE STEALER

After becoming Supreme Commander of Allied Forces in the Pacific, General Douglas MacArthur established himself in Brisbane during World War II.

With him came large numbers of American servicemen on tours of duty, or periods of recreational leave, landing in most Australian cities. Young Australian women were flattered by the lavish attention paid to them by the neatly dressed and free-spending strangers, who spoke with an accent they had only ever heard straight from Hollywood at the 'moving pictures'.

...a series of heinous crimes during the autumn of 1942 irrevocably tarnished the reputation of the US forces...

However, a series of heinous crimes during the autumn of 1942 irrevocably tarnished the reputation of the US forces in Australia.

The first victim was 40-year-old, Ivy Violet McLeod, whose badly beaten and strangled body was found on 3 May in Albert Park. Six days later, 31-year-old Pauline Thompson was also found, strangled. Luckily, for police, a piece of vital evidence immediately surfaced. Witnesses had reported seeing, or rather 'hearing', Pauline Thompson not long before her death with a man...a man who spoke with an American accent.

Before police could make any serious inroads with their investigations, on 18 May the killer struck again. This time the victim was 40-year-old Gladys Hosking, slain in a street near her home. As with the previous two murders, Gladys was left half-naked, violently bashed and strangled. After it emerged that yet another woman had been assaulted by a man who spoke like an American, the net began to close on 23-year-old Edward Joseph Leonski, who was soon arrested at his Melbourne barracks.

Gladys Hosking

This shocked his colleagues—Leonski came across as a cheerful and relaxed young man. However, the native of New Jersey was a heavy drinker and it later emerged had been raised in a very dysfunctional home, with one brother incarcerated and another in a mental health institution.

Leonski confessed to the murders. His testimony was disturbing, admitting he had choked Gladys Hosking because she had a fascinating and lovely voice, and he 'wanted' that voice. He also went onto admit that he had choked Pauline Thompson because she was singing to him and he wanted to keep hearing her sing.

Clearly somehow unbalanced, he then confessed to the death of Ivy McLeod, and also admitted that he had told friends in the past he had 'two personalities, like Jekyl and Hyde'. A report by the Medical Board, however, said

...he had choked Thompson because she was singing to him and he wanted to keep hearing her sing.

Joseph Leonski

He was subsequently sentenced to death by an American military court.

he was not insane and never had been, despite his troubled upbringing.

He was subsequently sentenced to death by an American military court.

After his conviction and sentencing, Leonski was reported to say to his guard,

'Death is a wonderful thing. They say I had a severe sentence but I don't think so. I think I got out of it lucky with death.'

After 24 weeks in detention, on 9 November 1942, Leonski was hanged at Pentridge Prison.

In 1986 a film, *The Death of a Soldier*, starring James Coburn, was filmed about Leonski and his murderous rampage.

MORE TROOP TROUBLE

A lust-associated homicide also occurred in wartime Brisbane, at the time more a big country town than a city, before Pacific hostilities began in the 1940s.

In this unsavoury incident, someone kicked and bashed to death a part-aboriginal woman. Street lighting in all Australian cities was greatly reduced as a war economy measure, and it was in a dark laneway in a dimly lit 'brown-out' area where two young local men unexpectedly discovered the body of Doris Roberts on 19 June 1944. The woman appeared to be in her 30s and they found her partially naked with horrific injuries akin to someone having been run over by a truck.

...they found her partially naked with horrific injuries akin to someone having been run over by a truck.

Near the battered body was a hat with a distinctive blue emblem, identified as part of an American paratrooper's uniform. The deceased had been employed at nearby Nick's Café, where management and staff soon confirmed that, in a drunken state, Doris and a similarly intoxicated American soldier had fallen down the steps when they left the premises.

The swarthy American returned to the café a little later to ask for some medical attention to a cut on his face.

It was then discovered that two American servicemen had been questioned about their leave passes by American Military Police in nearby Elizabeth Street. Their passes had been collected and the name of the bareheaded American was listed as 'A. Fernandez', attached to the 42nd General Hospital in the suburb of Holland Park.

About five hours later, Private Avalino Fernandez was awoken in his quarters, and the 30-year-old American admitted to the assault. At first, he downplayed the seriousness of the attack, saying it was no worse than the beatings he inflicted on his wife 'in the old days.' He also revealed that the assault occurred because his victim asked for money after the pair had engaged in what he believed to be consensual intercourse. When Fernandez admitted he would not have attacked any white woman who demanded money for sex, there was no doubt that the crime was partly race-motivated.

> **...saying it was no worse than the beatings he inflicted on his wife 'in the old days.'**

The death penalty had been abandoned in Queensland and the cocky American was confident he would escape the ultimate penalty his countryman Leonski had suffered in Melbourne.

However, he was not tried under the auspices of the Australian courts, and a US Services court martial found Fernandez guilty of murder, sentencing him to death by hanging.

Surviving a suicide attempt while in cus-

tody, Fernandez went on to be hanged on 20
November 1944 in Papua New Guinea, where
the US Military had removed him to so that
the execution could be performed.

A FATAL DECISION

...Lawson was found guilty in 1954 of raping two of five models he had abducted...

When Leonard 'Lennie' Lawson was found guilty in 1954 of raping two of five models he had abducted, Judge Clancy strongly supported the death penalty for the Sydney commercial artist.

Despite this, Lennie had his sentence commuted to life imprisonment, further lessened to a custodial sentence of six years after the NSW Labor Government reduced his maximum sentence. Lawson was free again by late 1960, and, unfortunately, the leniency shown by authorities towards the personable sex offender would eventually result in fatal consequences.

Lawson was raised in a loving middle-class family in Wagga Wagga, where he topped his Intermediate class at the local secondary school. At the age of 15, the handsome and popular youth began work as an apprentice commercial artist in Sydney. He excelled in this field and soon became the illustrator for *The Lone Avenger* and *The Hooded Rider* series, highly popular comic books of the era.

Around that time, a more sinister side of Lawson's personality began to emerge.

He began sketching and selling pornographic images...with a twist.

Some of the woman he drew appeared to

be dead.

Lawson married his childhood sweetheart at the age of 19, with the young couple soon producing two sons and a daughter. The successful freelance artist opened a studio where he began to photograph beautiful young women.

On 7 May 1954, at the age of 26, he took five June Dally-Watkins photographic models into the Terrey Hills bush in north Sydney. In the peaceful bush setting, the supposed 'shoot' took on a sinister aspect— Lawson produced a .22 rifle and a hunting knife and tied ropes around the wrists and ankles of the terrified young women. He physically molested each of his victims after he cut away their clothing and gagged them with sticking plaster.

...Lawson produced a .22 rifle and a hunting knife and tied ropes around the wrists and ankles...

He then paraded naked before his captives before raping a 19-year-old in front of them. After then forcing a 22-year-old married victim to have sex with him, Lawson suddenly appeared remorseful about his actions, threatening to commit suicide. When some of his captives assured the rapist that nothing would be divulged about the rapes and abductions, Lawson relented and the group returned to Sydney.

Predictably, authorities were quickly informed about the multiple assaults, and by the time Lawson returned to his studio, police

...the 'reformed' Lawson gained release from his minimum-security prison,

were waiting to arrest him.

Following his trial, lucky escape from the death penalty and relatively short-lived incarceration, the 'reformed' Lawson gained release from his minimum-security prison, living initially with his parents at Moss Vale. His wife had left him during his time in custody and after his release, Lawson showed no inclination to connect with her or his children again...which, in light of what was to come, was a godsend.

By August 1961, Len Lawson had moved to the fashionable Sydney suburb of Collaroy where he resumed his career as a commercial artist. It was in this role that he first met 16-year-old Jane Bower and her mother. The trio regularly taking outings together and Lawson began working on a portrait of Jane. Five weeks after they first met, the attractive young woman agreed to meet Lawson at his home where work on the portrait was planned to continue.

There, Lawson made unwelcome advances on Jane, and when she resisted he struck her heavily on the head with a sand filled sock. He then tied the unconscious woman's wrists together and forcibly had intercourse with her. After the victim regained consciousness, she was strangled and a hunting knife was plunged deep into her chest. Finally, as though in some weird ritual of restitution, the serial sex offender wrote 'God forgive me, Len' with an eyebrow pencil on her stomach.

Lawson wrote a confessional letter to his parents before returning to Moss Vale and slept that night in his car. Early the next morning he arrived at the nearby local Church of England Grammar School, where the daily program was beginning. The fugitive hid in the school chapel and, when teachers and students arrived for Morning Prayer, he accosted them at gunpoint, threatening to tie them up and use them as hostages.

By then, police had been alerted. While a distracted Lawson watched their movements, the School Headmistress, Ms. Jean Turnbull, attempted to wrestle the gunman's rifle from him. During their fierce struggle, five shots were fired, with one of the bullets fatally striking Wendy Luscombe, a 15-year-old student.

At his trial, a resolute jury took a mere 17 minutes to find Lennie guilty of two counts of murder, for which he received life imprisonment.

Despite his incarceration, the predatory Lawson continued to be a dangerous menace to society.

In 1972, at a jail concert, he grabbed performing artist Sharon Hamilton around the neck, holding a knife against her throat. Fear-

The fugitive hid in the school chapel and, when teachers and students arrived...he accosted them at gunpoint...

...the assault was aborted when other inmates struggled with Lawson, finally subduing him.

ing an attempted jailbreak, police removed the audience of prisoners from the room, but the assault was aborted when other inmates struggled with Lawson, finally subduing him. Ms Hamilton required minor surgery for her throat wounds and sadly she never recovered from the ordeal, ending up in the notorious Chelmsford mental facility.

She eventually committed suicide, adding yet another to the list of Lennie's victims.

Lawson received an extra five years on his life sentence after pleading guilty to a malicious wounding charge and was transferred to the Grafton Maximum Security Unit for the remainder of his long prison term. He applied for day leave and, in 1994, for a determinant sentence.

Speaking with a reporter at the time, he said he believed he deserved some freedom as he was no longer a threat, although 'the rhythms of the city and its women' got to him.

His application was rejected.

Lennie Lawson died in jail on 29 November 2003 after spending 48 years behind bars. Several paintings, produced by this talented but dangerously flawed man still hang in Grafton prison to this day.

LONG WAIT FOR JUSTICE

At one stage, she studied teacher training, but Theresa Crowe had long ago abandoned a mainstream and conventional lifestyle.

The 22-year-old lived alone in a loft above and behind a boat building business in trendy Chapel Street, Prahran, and was a fixture on the Melbourne nightclub scene.

Theresa's favourite haunt was Chasers, which she frequented several nights a week. She was dubbed 'Blackbird', by those that knew her, due to her customary black clothing. Other patrons at Chasers became worried when she did not appear at the venue for six successive nights and, on 25 June 1980, two concerned young men entered her one room dwelling.

There they discovered her mutilated and naked body, wrapped in a blanket.

Someone had strangled Theresa before deeply cutting her body from the neck to the vagina. Various observers immediately linked the killing to some kind of satanic ritual. Initial pathology reports put the death as having occurred only 12-15 hours prior to the body being found, which threw investigators.

Why?

The potential suspect they wished to question over the murder, Malcolm Joseph

Various observers immediately linked the killing to some kind of satanic ritual.

Bonnie Clarke

...Theresa had in fact been dead five days...

Thomas Clarke, who had come into contact with Crowe at Chasers on several occasions, had a waterproof alibi for the period in which the pathologist believed Crowe had died.

However, unbeknownst to investigators, Theresa had in fact been dead five days, something the bitter winter cold and her unheated apartment, acting like a refrigerator, had helped conceal.

It would take the brutal rape of another woman in 1983 for police to finally nab Clarke. When they finally did, he claimed that Crowe's death by strangulation was accidental and that he had slit her body so callously merely to throw investigators. The jury noted his callous mutilation of the corpse, sentencing him to 15 years imprisonment, albeit for the lesser charge of manslaughter.

This, however, was not the end of the evil that Malcolm Clarke had perpetrated—he was soon to face much more-serious charges.

On 21 December 1982, six-year-old Bonnie Clarke (of the same surname but unrelated to the accused) had been raped and stabbed to death at her Northcote home, where it just so happened that at the time Malcolm Clarke was a boarder.

When Bonnie's mother, Marion, had awoken that morning just before Christmas, she looked in on her daughter, but did not disturb her as she appeared to be sleeping. Looking in again once she was ready for work, she discovered Bonnie was stone-cold. Further inspection revealed her to be dead.

Someone had digitally raped and suffocated the poor young girl, wiping her body down after the obscene incident to remove any evidence, and then stuffing her bloodied pyjamas between her bed and a wall, the hiding place obscured with pillows.

Given there was no sign of forced entry, police turned their focus on Bonnie's mother, who appallingly found herself the prime suspect. She was never charged and the investigation eventually lapsed.

However, cold cases have a way of finding their way back into the warmth of a potential prosecution. With the advent of DNA testing and a small piece of evidence (a greeting card from Bonnie Clarke to Malcolm Clarke when he had been a boarder in the Clarke home) collected during Theresa Crowe's murder investigations, police reopened the case in 2001.

An undercover officer, pretending to be a fellow gang member, duped Clarke into a confession. Clarke was swooped on and the police finally had their man.

In court, Clarke once again argued accidental death—that he had smothered the girl when she had awoken to her digitally raping

Marion Clarke

...stuffing her bloodied pyjamas between her bed and a wall...

her. The jury would not hear of it, sentencing him to life imprisonment, with a minimum of 25 years before being eligible for parole.

In 2006, Clarke's lawyers took the case to the Court of Appeals to contest the verdict and sentence on the grounds that the method via which the confession was obtained was illegal.

This was to no avail.

After deliberation, the court found that, although the confessions were obtained by deception, there was no duress or intimidation and that the confessions were voluntary.

Bonnie Clarke and Theresa Crowe's deaths could finally be laid to rest and the man who took away their lives left to ponder in prison the evil he had perpetrated.

...the method via which the confession was obtained was illegal.

STEALING AN IDENTITY...
AND A LIFE

Rachel Barber

Caroline Reed Robertson grew up in the 1980s in the idyllic, middle-class Melbourne suburb of Surrey Hills.

During this time, little did anyone suspect that somewhere within her, the seeds of a cold-blooded killer were slowly gestating.

The eldest of three, Caroline's parents divorced when she was 16. By this age, she was already filled with a self-loathing, both ferocious and mentally destabilising. She let her ill-feelings about herself and her life pour out into lists and letters to her father in which she described herself as ugly, fat, stupid, weird, unwanted, boring and pathetic.

...she described herself as ugly, fat, stupid, weird, unwanted, boring and pathetic.

These writings also described an unstable relationship with her mother, who had been diagnosed with depression at Robertson's birth. Once can clearly construe from her words that she took some twisted and unwarranted responsibility for her mother's mental state, writing at one point,

'Why didn't she just have an abortion? Sometimes it makes me sick to the stomach that I was produced out of her.'

Across the road from the Robertson's lived the Barber's.

They too had three girls, and although

they may not have been as financially stable as the Robertson's, their lives from the outside must have grated at the troubled soul of Caroline.

The girls all seemed beautiful and talented and the family was popular with neighbours and friends. Despite a five-year age difference, Robertson grew fascinated with Rachel, for whom the family had moved to Melbourne from the country so that she could pursue a career as a dancer. Robertson babysat the Barber children several times and even told the 12-year-old Rachel (when she herself was 17) that she wanted to be her best friend.

By the age of 20, Robertson was working for a telecommunications company and living in Prahran, and her fascination with Barber had tipped over into obsession to the point where, in notes she wrote, it appeared Robertson wanted to somehow become Barber.

She began forming a plan.

On the first day of autumn in 1999, as usual, Rachel went to dance school. After class, she parted with her devoted boyfriend, Emmanuel (Manni) Carella, telling him she was off to meet an old neighbour who had promised her a chunk of money to take part in a psychology study.

That old neighbour was, of course, Caroline Robertson.

...her fascination with Barber had tipped over into obsession...

At 6.40pm, a classmate of Barber's saw her and Caroline on the Glen Iris tram and thought it odd as she had never seen Rachel on that line before. Barber had met Robertson, picked up some pizzas and was taking her back to her apartment before they went to the 'study'.

There was no study.

Instead, Robertson strangled the young girl to death.

...Robertson strangled the young girl to death.

Within hours of Barber not returning home at the scheduled time, her concerned parents reported her missing to local police. For days they waited, hoping for news. During this time, Robertson hid Barber's body in her closet, before moving it to a Kilmore district property belonging to her father, where she buried the corpse.

She also, for some strange reason, called the Barber's household six days after killing Rachel and left her unlisted number, almost as though trying to draw suspicion to herself.

Police investigations finally led them to Barber's shallow grave and the net began to close in on Robertson. An arrest was made.

When the case reached the courts, it was fairly cut and dry.

Robertson had confessed to police, and yet pleaded not guilty. However, the extensive documentation of her plans to dispose of

Barber, and her twisted desire to become some pale imitation of her, were damning. Much to the relief of the Barber family, she changed her plea to guilty and there was little the judge and jury need do but convict.

Which they did, on 29 November 2000, sentencing her to 20 year's imprisonment with hard labour.

...Robertson was prone to bouts of self-mutilation and intense epileptic fits...

During her early days in prison, Robertson was prone to bouts of self-mutilation and intense epileptic fits (something she had always suffered from), but eventually she became almost enamoured of prison life, with authorities fearing she might become institutionalised.

Robertson went onto to seek leave to appeal the severity of the sentence. When confronted by an angry Elizabeth Barber in the courtroom, the convicted woman withdrew the appeal, two weeks before the hearing. She will be eligible for parole in 2014.

After years of psychological counselling and time to meditate on her crime, one can only hope she will emerge from prison a truly changed woman and not just the sick and superficial transformation she hoped the killing of an innocent woman would bring.

CHAPTER 9

PACK MENTALITY AND EVIL DUOS

A MALEVOLENT DUO

A wicked partnership developed when Kevin Gary Crump and Allan Baker met in prison in the early 1970s.

In late 1972, this unsavoury relationship would result in the deaths of two innocents.

Baker was released first, soon gaining employment as a farm labourer on the Morse family property, Banaway Station, near the NSW town of Collarenebri, over 300 miles north of Sydney. He and Crump were reunited in November 1972, and immediately, their crime spree began.

First up, the pair shot dead young cotton picker, Ian James Lamb, in an armed robbery attack near Narrabri, netting a mere $20 from the callous murder. They then returned to the Morse's.

Waiting in hiding for Brian Morse to drive away in the early morning, the malevolent pair emerged and abducted Virginia Morse at gunpoint. The mother of three was

Crump & Baker

...the accused, who sniggered together when sickening details of their crimes were revealed.

forced to accompany them to their campsite 190 kilometres away. Despite her impassioned pleas for mercy, they staked her to the ground, raped her, shot her dead and sickeningly molested the corpse again, before finally throwing her body into a nearby river.

A police manhunt began soon afterwards and, on 13 November 1973, a police officer received a head wound after an exchange of shots in a house raid at Cessnock. Before long, the fugitives' car became bogged at Woodville in the Hunter Valley, and Baker and Crump were apprehended.

On 20 July 1974, Crump made a full confession and the men were remanded for trial. Despite the confession, the defence put in a plea of not guilty to all charges, including the wounding of the police officer.

During proceedings, many in the court were appalled by the behaviour of the accused, who sniggered together when sickening details of their crimes were revealed. Justice Taylor was clearly disgusted with their attitude. When the jury handed down its guilty verdict, his condemnation of Crump and Baker was scathing.

Sentencing Baker and Crump, Justice Taylor said,

'For sheer cruelty, for callous indifference to suffering, for a complete disregard of humanity, for the complete absence of a spark of human decency, what you have done to this woman and to her children and to her husband is without parallel in my experience... you would aptly be described as animals and obscene animals at that.'

He added,

'I believe you should spend the rest of your lives in jail and there you should die'.

Taylor finished by telling the pair he would like to see the death penalty reinstated for crimes such as those they had committed.

While in custody, the pair were separated after they began a homosexual relationship behind bars. At different times, both men went to the NSW Supreme court for a redetermination of their life sentences, with Baker even publically announcing his sorrow at having committed the crime.

These attempts were, however, unsuccessful, so in 2004, Baker and Crump went to the High court to challenge the law that imposed a minimum 30 years for those sentenced to life with a recommendation that they never be released.

The court disagreed in a 6-1 verdict, with Justice Kirby the sole dissenter, and thus Justice Taylor's wish of them never living a life outside of prison for their heinous crimes was upheld.

'I believe you should spend the rest of your lives in jail and there you should die'.

PACK DOGS

Two males leapt out to confront her, dragging the struggling woman into the vehicle before speeding away.

The rape and murder of Anita Cobby by five predatory strangers shocked the nation.

In the hospital where she worked, Anita's caring manner was greatly admired by both patients and colleagues. The 26-year-old Sydney nurse had recently separated from her husband, but the split appeared amicable. Her life was still full of rich promise and she hoped to travel overseas to pursue her interest in art.

Then came the fateful summer evening of 2 February 1986.

Anita and some nursing friends had enjoyed dinner together in a city restaurant. Afterwards, at around 9.45pm, she was strolling to her parents' home from the Blacktown Railway Station when a stolen Holden sedan screeched to a stop nearby. Two males leapt out to confront her, dragging the struggling woman into the vehicle before speeding away.

The next day, on the outskirts of Blacktown, a farmer in a paddock discovered Anita's naked body. It was clear someone had sexually assaulted her before practically severing her head from her neck with what appeared to be a knife.

Neville Wran, the NSW Premier, had met Anita when she was an entrant in a beauty contest, and in a state of shock promptly offered a government reward of $50 000 for information leading to convictions of those responsible for the crime. It appeared that Ms Cobby had been the unlucky random choice of a group of sexual predators, unknown to her.

Anita Cobby

By 17 February, police received information linking 20-year-old John Travers to the abduction and murder. The young man, raised in a dysfunctional environment, already had a long history of violent and deviant behaviour, including the bashing of homosexuals and the sexual abuse and killing of animals. His dominant personality resulted in other unsavoury characters replicating his acts of sexual aggression.

Police believed that Mick Murdoch, the slavishly loyal 19-year-old companion of Travers, and 22-year-old Les Murphy had stolen the white Holden used to abduct Anita Cobby. The trio admitted to the car theft, but denied any knowledge about the young woman's rape and murder. Further questioning implicated two other members of the Murphy family, with 29-year-old Gary and 34-year-old Michael joining the others as prime suspects.

The trio admitted to the car theft, but denied any knowledge about the young woman's rape and murder.

The Murphy family were known to police, with Michael having escaped from Silverwater prison in December of the previous year while serving a 24 year sentence for armed robbery, breaking into properties, and stealing, larceny

Les Murphy

and escaping from custody.

At first, little conclusive evidence could be gleaned from the five men, but a woman dubbed 'Miss X' unexpectedly provided crucial new information. The new witness knew Travers well, and she confided to police her belief that this young man was capable of committing a sex-oriented murder.

The breakthrough that police needed came when Travers admitted to 'Miss X' that he had murdered Cobby due to the fact that she had heard his name mentioned by the other perpetrators during the many sexual attacks she was forced to endure.

'We all talked about it,' confided Travers, 'but I was the only one with the guts to do it.'

Once this revelation occurred, the investigation gathered fresh momentum. Les Murphy revealed where the stolen car used in the abduction was hidden in Blacktown and Murdoch confirmed it was Travers who ended the victim's life by cutting her throat.

The five men were charged with abduction, rape and murder...

The five men were charged with abduction, rape and murder and, during their 12-week trial, sickening details emerged about their combined guilt.

They had been drinking heavily and smoking marijuana before their victim was randomly chosen and constantly raped by all five. It was also believed that, although beaten nearly to a pulp, Cobby had been alive when Travers decided to end her ordeal. His horrific termination of her life was via slitting her throat from ear to ear—cutting the top of her Adam's apple, opening her mouth from below, destroying almost all the muscles, nerves and veins on the right side of her face, severing the windpipe, cutting the right ear in three places and exposing her spinal canal.

A sixth man, Raymond John Paterson, was also implicated in the case for having aided and abetted the Murphy brothers when they went into hiding after the murder.

Travers did not face trial, pleading guilty before the case was heard.

The remaining four showed no remorse for their callous actions and the court displayed no leniency.

It would come as no surprise that loud applause broke out in court after when the others were found guilty of all charges, and sentenced by Justice Victor Maxwell to life imprisonment for the terms of their natural lives.

His horrific termination of her life was via slitting her throat from ear to ear...

COPY CAT HORROR

Two years after the Anita Cobby murder, Sydney reeled once more in disbelief at another abduction, rape and murder, this time by a group of even younger assailants.

The gang members were a bunch of street-living misfits and had only known each other for a matter of hours before they collectively decided to abduct and rape a young female stranger. During their short time together, it was the youngest member who assumed leadership of the gang and, despite his angelic-sounding name, 14-year-old Bronson Blessington's background was far from heavenly.

In his deprived home environment, four male adults had sexually abused the young boy, and in his life on the streets, he was an alcoholic who frequently sniffed petrol. The youngest of the five, it was Blessington who first suggested 'getting a sheila and raping her'.

The rest of the depraved gang were also from a variety of mostly disadvantaged backgrounds.

Fifteen-year-old Wayne Wilmott had been in trouble with law enforcement agencies since the age of five and his 'girlfriend', who he had met just hours before their callous crime, was mildly-intellectually-disabled, Carol Ann Arrow, a 17-year-old runaway. Matthew Elliott

...they collectively decided to abduct and rape a young female stranger.

was placed in the bottom 4% of the population in terms of intellect, while the unfortunate ape-like features of the last member of the gang, 23-year-old Stephen 'Shorty' Jamieson, caused him to be ostracised.

Janine Balding

On 8 August 1988, this group of fringe-dwellers decided the horrible fate of a popular, hard working, soon-to-be-married young woman—20-year-old bank teller, Janine Balding.

Balding had completed her working day at a Sydney bank and was approaching her vehicle in the Sutherland Railway Station car park when a gang of youths gathered menacingly around her. The terrified young woman was bundled into her car, which sped off down the F4 Freeway.

While Wilmott drove, Elliott raped Balding at knifepoint in the back seat. After the car screeched to a stop, the other males in the group raped her repeatedly while Wilmott and Arrow enjoyed their own sexual interlude in the now stationary car. The powerless victim was then dragged to the edge of the nearby Minchinbury Dam where her head was held under water until she drowned. Elliott later sold Balding's stolen engagement ring while the others used a credit card stolen from the deceased to access $300 from an ATM.

A social worker in contact with some

...her head was held under water until she drowned.

members of the group became suspicious about Blessington and Elliott's behaviour. Police were notified and, under questioning, the teenage pair made admissions. They accompanied investigators to the dam, from which Balding's body was recovered.

Along with Willmott and Arrow, the four maintained that the missing member of the group they knew as 'Shorty' was responsible for the murder. Blessington further added that Mark 'Shorty' Wells was the culprit's full name, but this well-known devil worshipper had an alibi, which passed official scrutiny.

Despite investigators' strong belief that Jamieson was the missing perpetrator, two of the others charged have maintained to this day that it was another 'Shorty', and not Jamieson, who wore a black headscarf when he participated in the abduction. Regardless, a fortnight after Janine Balding's body was discovered, Stephen 'Shorty' Jamieson was arrested in a Southport park on Queensland's Gold Coast.

Finally, all five suspects were in police hands, accused of theft, abduction, rape and murder.

Wilmott and Arrow consequently had their murder charges withdrawn, but were later convicted of abduction and theft. Wilmott received a custodial sentence of ten years, while Arrow was jailed for 18 months and

...this well-known devil worshipper had an alibi, which passed official scrutiny.

placed on a three-year good behaviour bond.

When they faced court in 1990, Blessington, Jamieson and Elliott showed no obvious remorse for their despicable crimes, with Blessington often mouthing obscenities to the press gallery during the hearings. Jamieson also consistently and stridently maintained that he was in no way involved with the crime, in line with other gang member who supported this.

Regardless, all three were found guilty and during his closing summary Judge Newman described the case as,

'One of the most barbaric killings in the sad criminal history of this state.'

Despite their youth, each received life prison sentences without parole, with Blessington becoming the youngest criminal ever, at least since our convict forebears, to have such a heavy sentence meted out upon him.

During his time in custody, Bronson Blessington became a devout Christian and model prisoner. Both he and Jamieson received unexpected, if short-lived, parliamentary support, from former NSW Labor Upper House member, Peter Breen, who passionately supported their claims of innocence.

Breen produced a book, *Life as a Sentence*, the contents of which included the following revelation,

'I love "Shorty" Jamieson. I'm not afraid

> **'One of the most barbaric killings in the sad criminal history of this state.'**

to say it.'

Then NSW Premier, Morris Iemma, described this extract as being 'a sickening tribute'. He ignored Breen's claims of misrepresentation by the Sydney press and eventually persuaded the gang's champion to resign from the Labor Party.

During the initial trial, Jamieson was found guilty of anally raping Janine Balding, but subsequent DNA testing revealed that neither Jamieson nor Wells was guilty of that particular crime.

In late October 2007, lawyers representing Jamieson applied for permission from the NSW DNA Review Panel to forward evidence relating to the case for testing by the Forensic Science Service laboratories in Birmingham, England. The lawyers wanted the scarf used by the attackers to gag Janine Balding during the sexual assaults. This request caused much debate in the NSW Parliament, with many Members not wishing to traumatise the Balding family by effectively reopening the case.

The lawyers wanted the scarf used by the attackers to gag Janine Balding during the sexual assaults.

Nothing came of this appeal, and lawyers representing Jamieson appear now to have unsuccessfully used all available legal appeals for their client, but are apparently still endeavouring to gain a judicial inquiry into his conviction.

Elliot and Blessington were offered a

momentary glimpse of the hope for freedom in 2007 when a missing staple in their court file gave them the opportunity for a fresh appeal. This sloppy record keeping in the Court of Criminal Appeal registry led to the pair being given special leave to take their case to the High Court, with the only good to come of this incredible blunder being the tightening of laws in NSW to ensure such never happened again.

When their case reached the High Court, it was unanimously dismissed, and the sentencing judge's recommendation was found not to amount to a formal court order against which an appeal could be based.

'Subsequent legislation affecting the position of Mr Elliott and Mr Blessington did not create any miscarriage of justice in the 1992 CCA (Court of Criminal Appeal) decision which would call for interference in that decision,' the High Court said in a summary of its ruling.

This effectively exhausted any chances for freedom for Blessington and Elliot who will now remain behind bars until their deaths.

And the others of the gang?

Wayne Wilmott became a dangerous repeat offender. After serving eight years for the abduction and rape of Balding, he returned to prison only two years later,

...Blessington and Elliot will now remain behind bars until their deaths.

...he received a custodial sentence of 36 years for his multiple rape offences.

following the attempted abduction of another young woman. A DNA jail-testing program in jail revealed the grim news that Wilmott was the man who kidnapped and raped a 19-year-old woman from the Leightonfield railway in Sydney's west in 1998. In 2005, he received a custodial sentence of 36 years for his multiple rape offences.

Carol Didden, nee Arrow, served her time, eventually marrying and blending away into a mainstream life. She came briefly to public prominence again when in 2006 she made a statement to police positively identifying Jamieson as being involved with the crime. This was 'for the sake of Janine's mother, Bev Balding' who she believed had the right to have this confirmed, and to end Barry Breen's relentless pursuit of 'justice' for Jamieson.

LUST AND VIOLENCE
IN THE OUTBACK

Brendan and Vester Fernando were two aboriginal youths who regularly attracted the attention of local police in the northern New South Wales town of Walgett.

By the time he reached his early 20s, Brendan had been a heavy user of marijuana and heroin for more than a decade. Petrol sniffing was also one of his indulgences and it seemed this dangerous habit may have caused him brain damage. His IQ rating was low, at about 60, and he was habitually spaced out on drugs, alcohol and medication.

His cousin, Vester, was a year older and had been an alcoholic since the age of 16. Both men had served several jail terms for violent offences.

In the late evening hours of a December evening in 1994, the boys were predictably out of control. Around 11.30 pm, Vester threatened to kill another indigenous youth with a machete. The two cousins then made their way to the local hospital car park, where they hoped to steal a vehicle.

During the attempt, they observed Sandra Hoare standing near a window inside the geriatric ward. The 21-year-old, engaged to a local police officer, had commenced her nursing

...made their way to the local hospital car park, where they hoped to steal a vehicle.

career in Walgett just two days earlier.

The Fernandos, fearing she had been a witness to their attempted theft, burst into the hospital premises, where they bashed an elderly patient and threatened the young nurse with a machete before abducting her.

Hoare was then led through the darkness to the local football oval where she was bashed and stripped before Brendan held her down while his cousin raped her. After her assault, Vester finished the job, decapitating the nurse with the machete.

The next day a massive search began for the missing woman, resulting in the discovery of her mutilated body that afternoon, her head separate from her trunk and stashed in an anthill. The battered hospital patient issued police with a description of the suspects and racial tensions escalated throughout the district after several aboriginal camps and houses were raided at gunpoint.

Fortunately, police gained vital information they needed before the situation grew worse. Another local aboriginal threatened earlier that evening by the cousins implicated them in the murder. Brendan was soon arrested and two days later Vester was apprehended at his sister's home 300 kilometres away in Dubbo. Cassette tapes from a stolen car were found in his possession and the Fernando

> **After her assault, Vester finished the job, decapitating the nurse with the machete.**

cousins were charged with murder.

Justice Abadee recommended both young men never be released after they received a life imprisonment sentence on 21 August 1997. It was the harshest sentence ever imposed on indigenous criminals in Australia.

Two years later, Vester stabbed his cousin Brendan to death in Lithgow Prison after he ascertained that Brendan had lied in statements to police. Since then, he has been confined in the High Risk Management Unit at Goulburn Jail, where he has embraced the Islamic faith, along with several other prisoners.

...Vester stabbed his cousin Brendan to death in Lithgow Prison...

NEVER RIDE WITH STRANGERS

They two young women were average high school teens.

It was the Labor Day long weekend in 1997 and the girls had decided to walk to a party along a lonely stretch of the Snowy Mountain Highway. Around 10 pm, they accepted a lift in a car from two strangers.

They were not to know that this would be the last car ride they would ever take.

They were not to know that this would be the last car ride they would ever take.

The unlucky teens were 14-year-old Lauren Barry and 16-year-old Nichole Collins. Their families had become close friends after they settled at Kalaru near Bega, close to the NSW South Coast, and Lauren and Nichole were constant companions. On the night they disappeared, they celebrated Nichole's approaching birthday with a couple of bourbon-and-cokes.

Three days later, Lauren's semen-stained shirt was found near the old Walagoot Road at Bega, the only clue to the girl's disappearance the task force would uncover for the next three weeks. As the days dragged on, reports came in about a cream and yellow sedan being sighted in the Tathra area around the time the girls vanished, but no definite leads resulted at the time.

It would be later discovered that the men travelling in that vehicle were repeat sex offenders, one of who had been recently ill-advisedly set free.

Twenty-eight-year old Leslie Camilleri's criminal life began early.

Lindsay Beckett

Described as an 'uncontrollable child', he had lived on the streets of Kings Cross from the age of 10 to 12, then been placed in a boys home 'til the age of 15. By late 1997, he had racked up 146 convictions, some of which were for sex offences, and had recently appeared in the Queanbeyan Court before Judge Fred Kirkman to answer six charges of sexual penetration of an 11-year-old girl.

Shortly before these serious charges were heard, the NSW Police Minister voiced strong opinions to the media as to how he thought sex offenders should be punished. In light of this, Camilleri's legal representatives argued the Minister's comments were prejudicial to their client's right to a fair trial. This plea worked, with Judge Kirkman declaring the case aborted and Camilleri free—unfortunately, in this case, free to go on to commit an even more heinous crime.

The second culprit was 23-year-old New Zealand-born Lindsay Beckett, also with repeat convictions for sexual crimes and theft, and a reportedly below average IQ. He met up

By late 1997, he had racked up 146 convictions, some of which were for sex offences...

with Camilleri in the town of Yass, where the two embarked upon a series of petty crimes.

Nineteen-year-old Rosamari Gandarias was their 'warm-up' for the Bega killings.

After picking her up near Canberra, they held her for 12 hours, during which they threatened her with a knife, beat and raped her. At a rest area near Bowral, she escaped into the bush and, given what would transpire a few weeks later, it is almost certain this escape saved her life.

On the night of 5 October, the men were travelling to Bega to visit Camilleri's de facto wife. They were high on alcohol and amphetamines, spoiling for trouble. Seeing the two young women, they stopped and offered them a ride, saying they were on the lookout for parties going on in the region.

Beckett produced a knife and ordered them to 'do what Les says'.

The girls at first went with it, maybe a little off their guard given the alcohol they had consumed, but it soon became clear that danger was looming when Beckett produced a knife and ordered them to 'do what Les says'.

What followed for Lauren and Nichole was nine hours of living hell.

During this time, the men would drive for a period, stop the car, rape the girls either orally or vaginally, then start again til the mood came over them to pull over and rape one or both of the girls again.

234

In the early hours of 6 October, they pulled over for the last time. The men separated the girls—Nichole was gagged and tied to a tree, while Beckett took Nichole to nearby Fiddlers Green Creek, where he attempted to drown her. When she struggled, knocking him into the water, his fury rose and he stabbed her several times until she died.

Beckett then brutally murdered Nichole, slashing her throat several times and, as she struggled in the throes of death, he stabbed and kicked her until the life left her body.

Covered in blood, Beckett changed into clean clothes and the depraved pair returned to Canberra. When they reached the nation's capital, the knife used in the gruesome murders was thrown from Commonwealth Bridge into Lake Burleigh Griffin, and the men then thoroughly cleaned the car before burning Beckett's bloodstained clothes.

The villainous pair may have escaped undetected. However, their nefarious pasts would be their undoing. Several weeks' later, police took them in separately for unrelated crimes. A map of Bega found in Beckett's cars was enough evidence for them to call in the Bega special taskforce.

Beckett finally admitted to the joint killings and on 12 November accompanied police to where the two bodies were located just a

When she struggled, knocking him into the water, his fury rose and he stabbed her several times until she died.

short distance apart. The following day, police divers recovered the murder weapon and a week later over 4000 people attended a memorial service for the girls in Bega.

On 26 June 1998, Beckett pleaded guilty to two counts of murder. Just under two months later, Supreme Court Justice Frank Vincent sentenced Beckett to two sentences of life imprisonment (to be served concurrently) with a non-parole period of 35 years, after which he was to be deported to New Zealand.

Camilleri plead not guilty, taking his chances at trial in the Victorian Supreme Court in February 1999. He was found guilty by a jury and on 27 April sentenced to two terms of life imprisonment without the possibility of release on parole.

Justice Vincent noted,

'Through your own actions, you have forfeited your right ever to walk among us again.'

'Through your own actions, you have forfeited your right ever to walk among us again.'

Although it is a fairly unique position to serve life without parole, despite not having physically killed anybody, Camilleri was judged to have been part of a criminal enterprise that resulted in the girls' murders. He appealed against his sentence on various grounds, but on 7 March 2001, the Victorian Supreme Court of Appeal rejected his appeal.

A further appeal was made to the High Court on 3 May 2002. This was promptly dismissed, leaving Camilleri with no further avenues of appeal.

CABIN 182

Dianne Brimble

With some weird sense of premonition, she experienced bad dreams in the days before the trip...

In late September 2002, 40-year-old Brisbane mother of three Dianne Brimble embarked on a P& O South Pacific cruise, accompanied by her sister, two of their children and some friends.

Brimble had been divorced from Mark Brimble, the father of her boys, since the late 1980s and was in a long-running on-again off-again relationship with David Mitchell, the father of her 11-year-old daughter, Tahlia. With some weird sense of premonition, she experienced bad dreams in the days before the trip, something she related to a friend, who passed it off as fear of the unknown.

If only Diane had heeded this eerie warning.

Brimble spent her first afternoon onboard ship getting to know the layout and meeting some of her fellow passengers. Eventually, she fell in with a group of eight men from Adelaide with who she began drinking. Others who met or spoke to her, including a security guard, claimed she was in high spirits, if a little intoxicated.

Sometime after 11.00pm, she returned quickly to her cabin to freshen up before hitting the ship's disco, the Starlight Club, which opened at 11.30pm. Stumbling in, she changed her shoes, and gave Tahlia a kiss goodnight, then was gone.

Sadly, this would be the last time Tahlia would see her mother alive.

Less than 12 hours later, Dianne Brimble was pronounced dead in cabin 182 when medical staff attempted to resuscitate her but were unable to do so.

After the ship's officers were informed there had been a fatality, security staff appeared to adopt an ill-advised 'damage control' strategy, initially announcing that a passenger had died of a heart attack. Surprisingly, the potential crime scene was not secured and the male occupants of cabin 182 were allowed to remove their belongings before investigation procedures began.

Who were these men?

Thirty-three-year-old Mark Wilhelm, 45-year-old Dragan Losic, 41-year-old Lettorio 'Leo' Silvestri and 29-year-old Peter Pantic— the group she had been seen leaving the Starlight Club with at around 4am.

The men quickly became 'of interest' to police, as did their four other companions, and it soon surfaced that five of the eight had criminal records.

Losic, father of three, a known bikie and ken do master, had escaped a rape conviction at the age of 18. He had 27 criminal convic-

Brimble was pronounced dead in cabin 182 when medical staff attempted to resuscitate her...

...Wilhelm had previously been fined in Australia for producing illegal drugs...

tions and two jail sentences, including three and a half years for drug offences. At the first night cruise disco, he received a warning from security guards for his offensive behaviour. His friend Wilhelm had previously been fined in Australia for producing illegal drugs and in the past Silvestri had been charged with drug possession and fraud.

Over the next few years, ongoing investigations into the matter would slowly unravel what had happened to Brimble, leading to a full coronial inquest.

One of the leading pieces of evidence lay in the large dose of the party drug, GBH, or Fantasy, found in Brimble's bloodstream during the post mortem. It was no coincidence that later in the night some of the men in question offered the same drug to other women they were trying to seduce.

Then there were the photos.

Supposedly taken by Wilhelm, these showed him and Brimble engaging in sex, also implicating another of their party, Ryan Kuchel, who passed out in the cabin during the night's activities. Wilhelm went on to claim that Brimble enjoyed consensual 'romps' with both Silvestri and himself, before she lost consciousness, although Silvestri argued he had no recollection of the oral sex she had performed on him. He would later notoriously go on to tell police in his interview that Ms Brimble was an 'ugly dog' who smelled, making it clear he didn't talk to 'anything that's over 60 kilos'.

Photos taken after Diane Brimble passed out were particularly horrific. In them can be seen a clearly vulnerable naked woman, unconscious or possibly dead on the floor, partly covered by a sheet, and having defecated herself.

DNA results became available from skin samples discovered under the deceased woman's fingernails, and Australian homicide officers resumed further investigations.

At the inquest into Brimble's death in 2007, Wilhelm asserted that he tried to resuscitate her after he found her lying on the floor of his cabin. He also placed her under a shower and when she still failed to respond, notified the ship's officers. Wilhelm reiterated that the sex interludes with Silvestri and he were consensual, with the latter claiming Brimble had attempted to rape him.

Other evidence aired at the inquiry contradicted these claims.

It was stated that Dianne Brimble was the victim of a pack rape after she consumed substantial quantities of the illicit sex drug, GBH. The damaging toxicology report indicated that the amount of the drug found in her body was three times the quantity one would expect to find in a recreational user's system and it was

Wilhelm asserted that he tried to resuscitate her after he found her lying on the floor of his cabin.

> **...toxic amounts of alcohol and the fantasy drug caused her fatal heart attack.**

concluded that toxic amounts of alcohol and the fantasy drug caused her fatal heart attack.

In late July 2007, after 66 days, the coroner finally referred the case to the NSW Director of Public Prosecutions with the assertion that a person or persons had contributed to the woman's undignified end.

Over a year later, on 11 September 2008, the NSW Director of Public Prosecutions announced that Mark Wilhelm, Lettorio Silvesti and Ryan Kuchel would all face charges. Wilhelm was expected to be tried for manslaughter and supplying a prohibited drug. The other accused would answer charges of perverting the course of justice and hindering police investigations.

Recent developments gave hope to Dianne Brimble's family that there would be a just closure to this frustrating case. Leo Silvestri was persuaded to plead guilty to the lesser charge of concealing a serious indictable offence. This change of heart, together with his undertaking to provide evidence against another of the accused, resulted in Silvestri receiving a suspended sentence of 15 months imprisonment. He was also placed on a 15-month good behaviour bond.

Ryan Kuchel, who informed police that his besieged friend Mark Wilhelm had become a suicide risk following the demise of Dianne

Brimble, was also given a suspended sentence after pleading guilty to the charges laid.

When Wilhelm finally faced a jury on counts of manslaughter and drug supply in October 2009, the trial hit some rough waters for the prosecution. Justice Howie instructed the jury to disregard the tasteless photos taken of Brimble by Wilhelm and to ignore his behaviour, 'as distasteful as it is, as reprehensible as it might be.'

The prosecution also dropped a significant element of the manslaughter case against Wilhelm—that of gross criminal negligence—deciding instead to press ahead with the charge that Wilhelm killed Diane Brimble by an unlawful and dangerous act in giving her an illegal substance potentially linked to her eventual death.

Sadly, for her family, after almost five full days of deliberations, the jury foreman delivered the gut-wrenching news that they were hopelessly deadlocked, unable to reach a majority verdict on both counts.

They were dismissed and Wilhelm walked free.

Although legal observers believed a retrial was unlikely, in early November 2009, the Department of Public Prosecution in NSW announced it would be seeking a retrial on both charges, scheduled for court in April 2010.

...the jury foreman delivered the gut-wrenching news that they were hopelessly deadlocked...

... a night of cruise-ship fun that turned into a nightmare her family can't escape.

Thus there still remains some hope for the chance of justice for the woman who might still be alive today were it not for a night of cruise-ship fun that turned into a nightmare her family can't escape.

SECTION SIX

STAND BY YOUR MAN

Sometimes its hard to be a woman
Giving all your love to just one man
You'll have bad times
And he'll have good times
Doing things that you don't understand

Tammy Wynette

Love is a binding force, for good or bad, and some women will stand by their men, regardless of the consequences...
...And do whatever it takes to protect him.

SECTION SIX

STAND BY YOUR MAN

CHAPTER 10

WIVES AND GIRLFRIENDS

LOVE ON THE INSIDE

A court psychologist described Heather Parker's feelings for career criminal Peter Gibb as a 'pathological infatuation' when both faced various criminal charges relating to Gibb's escape from legal custody.

The year was 1992.

Heather Parker had been a prison warden for three years before she met Gibb at the age of twenty-nine at the Melbourne remand centre. Her own marriage was falling apart and, before long, the mother of two was completely infatuated with the 38-year-old hardened crim, whose long criminal career included convictions for manslaughter and armed robbery. Since first incarcerated at 17, Gibbs had spent only 22 months out of jail, and it appeared likely would soon start another stretch of up to 12 years duration behind bars.

Other prison wardens associated with Parker were

hostile about the romance that was obviously developing. After they observed Parker and Gibb sneaking together into a remand broom cupboard, the wardens staged a stop-work meeting, resulting in Parker being transferred, first to the security ward at St. Vincent's Hospital and then to a clerical position at head office. Staff members there also expressed concern after Parker was discovered in a segregated area containing internal security reports.

By then, Gibb and another hardened criminal, Archie Butterly, were planning an escape from the remand centre. Parker readily agreed to assist them. In this role, she persuaded underworld contact, Alex Thompson, to steal a station wagon, a four-wheel-drive and some false number plates. Parker also obtained an automatic pistol and three stun guns by mail order from America. The four-wheel-drive was then fitted out with camping gear, food supplies, mobile phones, bolt cutters, handcuffs and a camouflage net.

...smashed a window and used tied-together sheets to slide down the wall...

The breakout occurred ten days after Gibb received another long custodial sentence. At 6pm on Sunday 2 March 1993, a loud explosion rocked the remand centre. Gibb and Butterly smashed a window and used tied-together sheets to slide down the wall into nearby Latrobe Street, where a Ford Falcon was parked, ready for their use.

A series of mishaps, altercations and accidents followed—Butterly received quite serious injuries when the pair crashed their getaway car, Gibb's arm was broken by a baton in a skirmish with police, and a senior constable was injured in the same incident—all before the escapees successfully made their escape.

The fugitives met up with Parker at Frankston where the trio switched vehicles, using the four-wheel drive to head towards Gippsland, east of Melbourne. Due to Butterly's injuries, they stopped at the Latrobe Regional Hospital so he could receive medical attention, before proceeding northeast towards more remote areas.

Their first full day of freedom ended at the historic Gaffneys Creek Hotel.

Gibb entertained some of the locals with a few songs on a guitar, but the trio inexplicably became nasty after vacating the bar area in the early hours of the morning. They set fire to the room they had booked, and the heritage building, constructed in 1865, burnt to the ground.

They set fire to the room they had booked, and the heritage building, burnt to the ground.

News of the blaze brought police rushing to the area.

An intensive search began and by noon on 13 March, police found the four-wheel-drive concealed in ferns at Picnic Point, about 25 kilometres from Gaffneys Creek. Police dogs resumed tracking the area before sniffing out Parker and Gibb, who fired on the search party, leading to a gun battle. Cornered and waist-deep in the nearby Goulburn River, Gibb surrendered quietly to police, but an aggressive Parker strongly resisted arrest.

Later, police found the body of Archie Butterly nearby, a bullet wound behind his left ear. To this day it remains unclear who killed him. Gunshot residue found on Parker's hand when police apprehended her pointed towards her as the shooter, yet, contrary to this, the revolver used in the killing was identified as the weapon stolen by Gibb from Senior Constable Treloar on the day of the breakout.

...police found the body of Archie Butterly nearby, a bullet wound behind his left ear.

Gibb and Parker were charged with six counts of attempted murder and 23 other criminal counts, receiving ten years imprisonment, with Parker's non-parole period set at six years and six months. Gibb was not eligible for parole until he served eight years. Parker's sentence was reduced further on appeal and she ended up only spending four years in prison.

In their appearances in court, the couple showed every indication of being deeply in love. When Gibb was released, they lived together and Parker bore him two children.

However, not all was well in their relationship.

In 2007, Parker faced the courts once

more, this time for the bashing of a woman, Heather Gibbs in 2004. Parker punched Gibbs in the face, repeatedly struck her arm against a bench, hit her with kitchen stools and kicked her. Gibbs suffered a broken arm and spent six days in hospital. Parker's defence offered that she was in an abusive relationship with Gibb at the time, suffering post-natal depression and that there was no premeditation in the attack.

Parker received a 2 ½ years suspended sentence, allowing her to continue to care for her two young children and in a position to decide whether to stay with her literal 'partner-in-crime'.

> **Parker punched Gibbs in the face, repeatedly struck her arm against a bench, hit her with kitchen stools and kicked her.**

Heather Parker and Peter Gibb

RUSSIAN ROULETTE

John Killick

...a hijacked helicopter landed in the exercise yard of the heavily guarded premises.

In March 1999, high drama erupted inside the Silverwater maximum-security prison.

Seemingly, out of thin air, a hijacked helicopter landed in the exercise yard of the heavily guarded premises. A hail of bullets erupted as 58-year-old armed robber John Killick clambered aboard, but he escaped unscathed.

The daring rescue mission was a success.

This prison escape, as with that of Heather Parker, once more demonstrated the power of obsessive love, for it was Lucy Dudko, Killick's 42-year-old lover, who was behind the madcapped scheme.

Before meeting Killick, Dudko seemed to have it all.

Married to scientist Alex Dudko with who she immigrated to Australia in 1993, she was blessed with a young daughter and was studying for a doctorate in history at Macquarie University. Yet for all of this, she threw a seemingly idyllic life away for Killick, an ageing womaniser, permanently broke because of a chronic gambling addiction.

In 1999, three years into his affair with Dudko, Killick found himself in custody after robbing a bank and shooting at an off-duty police officer.

Desperate to be reunited with her love,

Dudko became the mastermind behind an audacious prison break.

She participated in a 'dummy run' in a helicopter ride two weeks before the actual breakout and purchased firearms to facilitate the escape. When the day of the jailbreak came, hiring a helicopter for a joy ride, she produced a sawn-off shotgun from her handbag and held it to the neck of the pilot, Tim Joyce.

In a scene not unlike something straight from an action movie, Dudko forced Joyce to land the chopper on an oval inside the maximum-security prison, then lifted her lover free amidst gunfire from prison officers, who eventually ceased firing when other prisoners tried to get in on the escape plan.

Initially, the fugitive couple eluded justice by relocating several times around the country. Finally, six weeks after the breakout, they were arrested in a Sydney caravan park. Killick received an extension on his original sentence and was returned to custody at Goulburn Jail. Dudko, dubbed 'red Lucy' by the Australian media, was sentenced to ten years in custody at Mulawa Women's Prison.

In court, Justice Helen Morgan questioned Dudko about her involvement, wanting her to explain the motivation for this seemingly out of character involvement in the jailbreak.

Dudko provided two identical reasons.

Lucy Dudko

...she produced a sawn-off shotgun from her handbag and held it to the neck of the pilot...

'First of all, I love him. Second, I love him.'

Dudko consistently claimed another woman participated in the raid from the air and, during her imprisonment, regularly complained about bad treatment. Regarded as a high-risk prisoner, 'red Lucy' was obliged to wear a conspicuous orange uniform when she received visitors. She was later moved to a minimum-security correctional centre where she served seven years before being released for good behaviour in 2006. The media swarmed about her on her release, but she disappeared without word, not wanting anything to do with them.

Banned from seeing Killick in the early years of her time in custody, Dudko regularly wrote emotional love letters to him, something it's believed she still does. It is also alleged that the couple had a marriage request refused in 2000.

They will not be reunited until at least 2013, when, at the age of 71, Killick will be eligible for parole.

Dudko now works baking pavlovas in a factory, ironically just a kilometre away from her daring jailbreak, and lives a quiet life, avoiding people where she can. She still refuses to comment about her relationship with Killick and what might transpire upon his release.

...'red Lucy' was obliged to wear a conspicuous orange uniform when she received visitors.

CHAPTER 11

GANGSTER 'MOLLS', MOTHERS, MADAMS AND MATRIARCHS

WENDY PEIRCE

No one would ever accuse Wendy Peirce of being shy.

During her turbulent de facto marriage with the late Victor Peirce, she also allegedly shared a brief relationship with Graeme Jensen, a close friend of her partner. An attempted police arrest of Jensen in October 1988 resulted in the career criminal's death. A few hours later, two young constables were notoriously executed in the infamous 'Walsh Street Shootings' in South Yarra. This double murder was believed to have been a revenge killing following the demise of Jensen near Narre Warren.

Victor Peirce and three other men were soon arrested and charged with the homicides, but were later acquitted. Wendy Peirce was placed (at considerable expense to the taxpayer) in a witness protection program as the Crown case against the four defendants relied heavily upon her evidence.

Victor Peirce

...she slashed another female across the face with a broken glass in a Melbourne hotel...

However, prior to her expected court appearance, Peirce changed her story, and the alibi she provided for her de facto husband helped cause the Crown's case to collapse. Shortly after, she was jailed briefly for perjury.

Years later, in 2005, after Victor Peirce became a victim of the Melbourne gangland war, Wendy Peirce came clean, admitting she had provided false evidence and that her late de facto husband had participated in the Walsh Street murders.

Wendy herself has never been adverse to violence.

Around the time of the Walsh Street trials, she slashed another female across the face with a broken glass in a Melbourne hotel and in July 2008 was charged with issuing threats to two women who allegedly had affairs with her late partner.

Currently 52, it would seem unfavourable publicity and a troubled existence follow closely, in no way diminishing the feisty woman who chose to spend nearly all her adult life with an incorrigible and dangerous criminal.

In late January 2009, Peirce was ordered to undertake 500 hours of community work after failing to pay a series of traffic offences, which over many years had escalated to over $14 000 in accumulated fines.

More-serious charges have since followed.

Around 5 pm on 28 March 2009, 44-year-old Mark Lohse received life-threatening wounds to the face when a group of people outside a Port Melbourne hotel viciously attacked him with a meat cleaver. Unfortunately for Lohse, he was mistakenly identified as Bob Sales, the father of the woman involved with the ex-boyfriend of Wendy Peirce's 23-year-old daughter Kate.

Following the assault, Wendy Peirce, Kate and Andrea Fuzzard were charged with attempted murder and intentionally causing grievous bodily harm. A 22-year-old Richmond man, Tong Yang, the alleged wielder of the cleaver, and hired for a paltry $200, was also charged.

Peirce, who the court learned was receiving treatment for depression, did not apply for bail at her April hearing and was remanded in custody. Kate Peirce was charged over the attack, while Yang was sentenced to six years imprisonment for his part in the crime.

Kate Peirce will never face the courts regarding this offence. In December 2009 she was found dead in her Greensborough home. The police said there was nothing suspicious surrounding the death and it is believed she died of a drug overdose.

At time of print, a family wrangle over the funeral and burial of Ms Peirce was in full

...a group of people outside a Port Melbourne hotel viciously attacked him with a meat cleaver.

swing, with Wendy wanting it held off for at least three months until she believes she will be freed.

Given Wendy Peirce was Kate's closest next of kin, it appears her wishes may be granted, although whether Wendy Peirce will be freed remains to be seen.

GRANNY EVIL

Sometimes the men who female characters of the criminal world stick by are not just their husbands or partners, but also their children.

Kath Pettingill, Wendy Peirce's de facto mother-in-law, is possibly the most infamous of these maternal types.

The well-known matriarch of a notorious criminal family has remained fiercely loyal to her offspring. Dubbed 'Granny Evil', the former brothel madam bore six sons who would go on to become notorious gangsters. Kath herself was interviewed in relation to Melbourne's Great Bookie Robbery, some of her sons were linked to the Russell Street bombing, and they were also associates of disgraced NSW detective Roger Rogerson. The Pettingill clan was closely linked to a group of notorious Melbourne criminals including Mark Militano, Frank Valastro, Graeme Jensen and Gary Abdallah, and the Moran boys, Mark and Jason.

Kath has lost several of her children.

Jamie, a heroin addict, died of an overdose at the age of 21.

Dennis Allen, dubbed 'Mr Death' by police, died of heart disease while awaiting charges for murder, with Kath on record lamenting he had died before she could shoot

Dennis Allen

...the former brothel madam bore six sons who would go on to become notorious gangsters.

Kath Pettingill

him herself. Connected to two murders, he could have been involved in as many as twelve. When he murdered Hells Angel biker Anton Kenny, Allen reportedly dismembered his unfortunate victim with a chainsaw. Allen also participated in at least 30 armed-robberies.

Two others of Kath's boys, Victor Peirce and Trevor Pettingill, were habitual criminals, strongly suspected of being involved in the Walsh Street shootings. Both Peirce and Pettingill had long-standing involvements in the illegal drug trade and it was well known that Victor was also an armed robber. A gangland execution in Port Melbourne ended his violent life, while Trevor Pettingill has served many custodial sentences for drug-related offences since his implication in the Walsh Street reprisal killings.

When Victor was taken out by other underworld figures, Kath said quite openly on radio she was determined to avenge his death, believing other criminals had shot him.

'If I had a gun at this moment, first of all I would get even'

'If I had a gun at this moment, first of all I would get even,' she said, showing her fierce devotion to her family.

She went on to say that she would have gladly taken the bullet for her son. Police immediately feared that a vast gangland battle would begin, and indeed, it did.

Her eldest, Peter, and his other brothers,

Trevor Pettingill and Lex Peirce, were regarded as Australia's most notorious gun and drug dealers in the 1980s, with Peter spending most of his life in prison on a variety of charges.

In retirement, the feisty matriarch moved to the peaceful Victorian coastal haven of Venus Bay. She retains a ghoulish sense of humour and a particularly Kath-inspired front door message allegedly greets any visitors to her home:

'Premises protected by shotgun three days a week. Guess which three!'

It is believed, as with so many other underworld figures, her life story will be played out on film or television as a bio-epic sometime in the near future.

What a story it will make.

'Premises protected by shotgun three days a week. Guess which three!'

ROBERTA WILLIAMS

Roberta Williams

In April 2007 what could only be described as a sadly pathetic incident reminiscent of a soap opera blazed out of control in Melbourne's Supreme Court.

Then 37-year-old Roberta Williams, ex-wife of major gangland figure, launched a tirade of invective against the much younger rival for her ex-husband's love, 21-year-old Renata Laureano.

Yet, for those who know Roberta's colourful past, this was just another minor disturbing episode of the many that have plagued her since she was a child.

Her father was killed in a trucking accident when she was an eight-month-old infant. According to Roberta, as she grew into childhood, at least two of her mother's subsequent de facto partners subjected her to physical abuse. Her own mother was apparently no better, meting out a violent brand of tough love—routinely whipping her with a jug cord, holding her head under the bathwater and locking her out of the house. In one particularly nasty episode when Roberta was nine or ten, her mother held her down and attempted to pour nail polish remover in her eyes as punishment.

Roberta's mother finally abandoned her,

...routinely whipping her with a jug cord, holding her head under the bathwater and locking her out of the house.

throwing her out of home—at the age of 11, she was a street kid, later becoming a ward of the state. It is interesting to note that Roberta's sister, Susan Mercieca, tells a very different tale of their childhood—a tale that almost entirely contradicts Roberta's own account, painting Roberta as a liar, selfish and money-hungry.

Renata Laureano

Roberta's own account of her supposedly vicious younger life, devoid of love, does fit with the fact that it warped the young woman's attraction towards men from the wrong side of the tracks.

At the age of 16, she formed a relationship with Dean Stephens, bearing him a child less than a year later, and two more during a relationship that became increasingly violent and abusive. At one point, she was so badly beaten with a handgun that, when her sister saw her injuries, she allegedly ran from the room and vomited. That beating, which happened after the couple had split, caused her a broken jaw, smashed nose, skull, cheek and eye socket fractures, and other bodily injuries.

...when her sister saw her injuries, she allegedly ran from the room and vomited.

According to Williams, 'The Footscray police couldn't believe the injuries. They took me to hospital and I was kept there for two weeks...the only reason I wanted to survive was for the kids.'

The twisted relationship between Roberta and Stephens ended in 1997 and the mother of three settled in Essendon. There, a year later she met her future husband.

Carl Williams.

Bearing him a child, she went on to live a life where she wanted for nothing, as Williams rode the amphetamine wave sweeping Australia. Roberta and Carl 'Fat Boy' Williams were effectively the king and queen of Melbourne's drug trade, pitted constantly against their archrivals, the Carlton Crew, with who they would engage in a bloody gangland war, later captured in the acclaimed television series *Underbelly*.

Like all relationships, her one with Williams had its highs and lows, but she remained fiercely loyal to him. The pair constantly bickered and were often separated when either or both were in prison, but the marriage somehow survived for nearly a decade.

However, once Carl received a crushing custodial sentence of 35 years for the multiple murders he had committed, the often-acrimonious marriage ended. Their relationship, however, did not. And yet despite Carl's new love interest and the friction between her and Roberta, she has admitted to still loving him, if not being 'in love' with her ex-husband.

It was reported in late 2007 that Roberta converted to Islam as the new man in her life was of the faith. She then went on to try and

> **Roberta and Carl 'Fat Boy' Williams were effectively the king and queen of Melbourne's drug trade...**

convince Carl to also convert, but to no avail.

In January 2009, her eldest son, Tye Stephens, was arrested near his mother's home in the Melbourne suburb of Ascot Vale, charged with committing a series of burglaries and thefts. This arrest indirectly caused Roberta to lose her BMW, which was repossessed by a finance company once her Ascot Vale address was publicised. Two months later, Tye was sentenced to time in jail for driving with a suspended licence and failing to appear on bail, and finally in August he pleaded guilty to the crimes.

Carl Williams

When appearing for sentencing before Judge Liz Gaynor in early December 2009, she described the crimes as 'high-end, professional offending'. As Stephens received four-and-a-half years' jail with a non-parole period of two years, Roberta apparently let out a loud sigh, swore and moaned.

Thus, despite an autobiography published in 2009 through which she tried to show the world the 'real' Roberta, Williams remains mired in the criminal world, maybe never to escape it.

...Williams remains mired in the criminal world, maybe never to escape it.

BARBARA WILLIAMS

Barbara Williams

Carl Williams was not allowed to attend his mother's funeral on 2 December 2008, but the convicted gangland murderer was an integral part of the farewell service honouring her life.

He put together an emotional tribute to her, written from the Barwon Prison cell where he is serving out a total of 35 years for multiple killings, mostly of other gangland figures, such as the Moran brothers.

Carl Williams depicted his mother as 'everything', describing her death as 'the hardest thing I ever had to deal with'.

He went on to say,

'There's nothing in the world I would not have done for you. I always looked so forward to ringing you up every morning and hearing your voice. You were my pillar of strength... you were my everything and I love you with all my heart.'

A photo of Carl and his mother, snapped during a once happy time, sat atop her white coffin and the service was recorded so that her son could watch the proceedings later in prison.

Her estranged spouse, George Williams, was given leave from his jail sentence under armed escort to attend the memorial service. There, he heard his former daughter-in-law,

...he is serving out a total of 35 years for multiple killings...

Roberta Williams, describe his wife of many years as,

'The mother I never had…she stood up to our enemies…because she thought that loyalty was a lifetime thing. She loved us unconditionally.'

Sixty-one colourful balloons (one for every year of Barbara Ann Williams' life) were later released outside the church, but there had been little brightness and cheer during this lifetime. Nine days previously, the woman who had lost one son, Jason, through a heroin overdose, and whose baby son and estranged husband were currently both serving jail sentences, found her wretched existence too hard to bear.

Barbara Williams took her own life in an apparent drug overdose.

In many ways, she would always just be Mrs Williams, son of Carl a former supermarket shelf-stacker, and wife of George. To most outward appearances she was a 'normal', nondescript resident of the north westerns Melbourne suburb of Essendon.

Unfortunately, for her, the men in her life were far from such.

Her husband had been on the police watch-list for years. Despite his seemingly benign appearance, and the conservative lifestyle he lived, he had been linked to the Moran family

Barbara Williams took her own life in an apparent drug overdose.

back in the '90s and was pegged as working in cahoots with son Carl, heading the 'family business'—drug trafficking between 2002 and 2004.

Police finally scored a conviction against him in 2007 and, despite a strong fight to keep him out of jail due to his deteriorating health, he was sentenced to 4 ½ years at Barwon Heads, the same facility housing his son.

Then there were her boys.

Her eldest Shane died of a drug overdose in 1997, and her youngest Carl headed one of the biggest gangs in Melbourne, integral in the undertaking of the biggest and bloodiest underworld battle the city had ever seen, for which he paid dearly via incarceration.

Despite her close criminal family connections, Barbara was no gangland matriarch in the vein of other famous Melbourne underworld clans. During the most heinous period of Carl's 'time at the top', it was reported by police that he would go to his mum's house for a simple home-cooked meal. It was also alleged that she acted as something of an ATM for him, hiding drug money in her home and then leaving it in wads in the letterbox for him when requested.

On his 29th birthday on 13 October 1999, she was at home when her son arrived with a bullet in his belly. He had just been shot

...hiding drug money in her home and then leaving it in wads in the letterbox for him when requested.

by Jason Moran. Some believe seeing her son in this state helped her push through the fact of the violence he was part of, with her seeing it merely occurring because he needed to protect himself.

Jason Moran

During Carl's trial, she turned up to court every day, possibly partially as a respite from only seeing her son manacled in prison garb on her visits to him during his confinement. When she heard he was ready to plea-bargain over murder charges involving the Moran brothers, Pasquale Barbaro and Mark Mallia, she begged him to resist, fearing she would never see her son free again, but to no avail.

In one of her few media appearances on the Channel 7 nightly television show, *Today Tonight*, she appeared up against Judy Moran in a mostly civil interview, although with each predictably blaming the other's families for the eight-year gangland war that ended the lives of close to 20 criminals in Melbourne.

When pressed, she was quick to defend Carl.

'He had to (kill) to save his family's lives because his family's lives were under threat by the boys, Jason and Mark.

'He was backed into a corner.

'It was kill or be killed.'

Tragically, for Barbara Williams, on the night of 22 November 2008, she would also

'He had to (kill) to save his family's lives...'

A flute of champagne and several bottles of sleeping pills...

end up 'backed into a corner', with the only answer available to her?

A flute of champagne and several bottles of sleeping pills, leading to an easy, if tragic, exit from her pain-filled existence.

MURDER ON

Des Moran

Less than a year and a half after the smash hit TV series *Underbelly* aired all around Australia (except Victoria, where it was delayed until later in the year for fear it might prejudice court proceedings involving characters depicted in the show), yet another gangland murder dominated the headlines, as did another gangland matriarch.

On Monday 15 June 2009, 60-year-old, Des 'Tuppence' Moran, the last living male member of the Moran clan, stopped for a coffee at his favourite cafe haunt, the Ascot Vale Pasta and Deli Cafe, like he did on any given day of the week.

At a minute before midday, two men clad in balaclavas, approached him.

Seconds later, he was dead with seven bullets lodged in his body.

Andrew Rule, co-author of the *Underbelly* books, said at the time,

'One thing about a lot of these fellows (referring to underworld figures) is that they are creatures of habit...Desmond made a habit of turning up to drink coffee at a particular deli in Union Road, they knew where to find him.'

Des was the brother of Lewis Moran, famously murdered in 2004 during Mel-

Seconds later, he was dead with seven bullets lodged in his body.

Judy Moran

Witnesses at the scene say they heard gunshots and saw 'a guy drop to the ground' as a car sped away.

bourne's gangland war, and uncle to Mark and Jason Moran, also killed during this time. Jailed in the 1980s for manufacturing amphetamines, Des kept a low profile after his release and was supposedly the most amiable of the Moran clan. According to John Silvester, another of the *Underbelly* writers, Des was 'too popular and too harmless to be placed on any hit list.'

Unfortunately, for Tuppence, someone had it in for him.

Little did he know how close to home was that person.

Witnesses at the scene say they heard gunshots and saw 'a guy drop to the ground' as a car sped away. Shortly after, well-known crime matriarch, 64-year-old Judy Moran arrived on the scene screaming, 'Oh Dezzie, Dezzie'.

However, those close to the Moran family found this outward display of supposed grief a sham, saying Judy and Des detested each other, and had done so for 20 years.

Des apparently blamed Judy for the jail sentence he received over interference with a court hearing—Judy generally disliked him, but the rift between them became irreversible when, despite having been separated from Lewis for years before his shooting, Judy believed she did not receive enough from his estate, including a sizeable share of Des and

Lewis's family home.

As Des was no doubt aware, Judy Moran was no woman to trifle with.

Overall, her life had been depressingly similar to that endured by her former adversary, Barbara Williams. Judy married career criminal Leslie 'Johnny' Cole at a young age. The marriage ended in divorce and in 1982 Cole became the victim of a Sydney gunman. (Mark Moran, executed outside his Melbourne home 18 years later by Carl Williams, was the son of Judy Moran and Leslie Cole.)

Lewis Moran

By the time Cole was murdered, Judy Moran was involved in a relationship with Lewis Moran, with Jason Moran born from this union. In 2003, Jason became yet another Melbourne gangland victim. Both murders were linked to the Williams clan.

The murder of her estranged husband followed in a Brunswick club a year later, this time under the command of another figure who would come to prominence not long after when he fled Australia to escape drug convictions—Tony Mokbel.

It may come as no surprise that a great deal of antipathy existed between Judy Moran and Roberta Williams, and some even speculate it is an important piece of the gangland puzzle as it predated the gangland war, being one of the reasons Carl Williams fell out with

...Jason became yet another Melbourne gangland victim.

Mark Moran

...he killed both Mark and Jason in separate incidents, leaving Judy both bereft and furious.

the Moran's in the first place.

As far back as the mid '90s, Roberta's first husband played football with the Moran boys, but the female members of the clan were not so forthcoming with Roberta, pushing her away. This was something she would never forgive them and apparently led to her next boyfriend, Carl Williams, being wary of the Morans, but not in a position to challenge them as he climbed the drug dealing ranks of Melbourne's underworld.

During an altercation in 1999 over money he allegedly owed the Morans, where he was nearly killed by Mark Moran, the stakes escalated, with Williams vowing to wipe them out. Good to his word, he killed both Mark and Jason in separate incidents, leaving Judy both bereft and furious.

Despite the death all around her, Judy seemed to revel in the high profile she had as a gangland widow, and out of the public eye was renowned for being a hard-nosed 'ballbreaker'— used to getting her own way no matter what it took. This became more difficult for her as the men in her life progressively became victims of the gangland wars, but it didn't stop her trying to sustain her 'caviar and *Cristal*' lifestyle.

Unfortunately, for Des, the one thing getting in the way of Judy's desire to maintain her high tastes…

Was him.

The shooting of 15 June was not the first attempt on Des's life.

In March 2009, while sitting in his Mercedes, someone fired a single shot through the front windscreen. The bullet narrowly missed him, lodging in the steering wheel. At the time, police said they were 'investigating a number of motives, but did not think it was related to the underworld war.'

When asked about the shooting, Moran said he had pleaded with the Commissioner of Victoria Police, Simon Overland, to allow him to carry a gun for protection, but Overland had refused. Moran argued that if he had had a gun he would have fired back at his assailant.

'I would have killed him or he would have killed me, one or the other.'

Following Des's death, Homicide and Purana squad members worked through the night to gather sufficient evidence to issue search warrants—after the first attempt on his life, they already had their suspicions.

Within hours of the killing, the police had unravelled details of the plot and the next day went on to charge Judy Moran and her friend Suzanne Kane (sister-in-law to Jason Moran) as accessories to the murder.

On Tuesday 16 June, Geoff Armour (also

'I would have killed him or he would have killed me, one or the other.'

under investigation for the previous attempt to kill Tuppence), partner of Suzanne Kane, faced an out of sessions hearing before a Portland Bail Justice where he was charged with murdering Des Moran. He was then transported to Warrnambool and held overnight before facing the Melbourne Magistrates' Court the following day. He did not apply for bail and is currently remanded in custody.

Police later also went on to arrest Michael Farrugia.

...Judy Moran deserted the getaway car containing a rifle and a gun-case...

At the same time the net closed around Armour, the usually glamorous Judy Moran arrived at the custody centre, clutching a walking stick, wearing purple tracksuit pants and a scruffy black jumper.

During the hearing, police told the court that, nine hours after the murder, Judy Moran deserted the getaway car containing a rifle and a gun-case on Mincha Street in Ascot Vale. She then dumped a pair of white knitted gloves into the bushes on Brunswick Road and calmly walked home. The homicide squad interrupted her walk, arresting her on suspicion of involvement in the murder. Judy's immediate defence was that the shooting had been extremely stressful and that a walk in the night air was her solution to de-stressing.

Police phone taps also revealed her discussing disposing of the items used in the murder with Kane and Amour in a crude code, referring to the getaway car as 'the dog' and how it was going to be dealt with. When police raided Moran's home they found three handguns, clothing matching the description of that worn by the gunmen, a wig and two sets of stolen number plates. Moran remained silent throughout the entire eight-hour hearing and thanked the bail justice when it ended.

In a bizarre twist of fate, Judy Moran's house was set on fire while she sat in custody that night, just hours after being charged as an accessory to murder. The chief prosecutor Gavin Silbert QC said a fire at Moran's home showed the 'major danger associated with this investigation'.

Police said they were treating the blaze as 'suspicious'.

Moran's house was set on fire while she sat in custody that night...

Both Moran and Kane faced the Melbourne Magistrate's Court on 18 June where it was revealed that a shotgun had also been found hidden under some cushions, loaded with six shotgun shells, ready for use. Detective Senior Constable Steven Reidy stated in court he feared Moran would flee overseas if she were released on bail. It was also beleivered that if Suzanne Kane were granted bail she would most likely flee to Western Australia. After much deliberation, Magistrate Jelena Popovic said she was concerned about the safety of members of the community, therefore refusing both Moran and Kane bail.

Victorian police commissioner Simon Overland said television scriptwriters would be hard-pressed to devise such a convoluted scenario.

'Fact is almost stranger than fiction with what we've seen,' Overland told ABC radio. 'If you were a scriptwriter and sat down and wrote this stuff you'd probably say it's a bit farfetched.'

Des Moran's funeral took place on 26 June 2009.

More than 300 people crammed into the Roselyn Court Homestead reception centre, among them gangland survivor Mick Gatto and prominent members of the racing community. Police established roadblocks around the reception centre and plain-clothes detectives monitored the service.

In the Melbourne Magistrate's Court on 21 July, despite Moran suffering from what a serious form of blood cancer, police escalated both the Moran and Kane charges of accessory to 'murder after the fact' to that of murder. Upon examining CCTV footage of the streets near the murder-scene, Purana detectives alleged both women played a part in the murder. The new charges claimed that Moran and Kane either conspired to kill Des

...police escalated both the Moran and Kane charges of accessory to 'murder after the fact'...

Moran or had prior knowledge of his murder. Ms Moran's lawyer, Brian Bourke QC, criticised police for their 'indecent haste' and said he was 'concerned about the sinister aspect of serving the charge of murder'.

All four are currently being held, pending a preliminary hearing sometime in 2010, but even in custody, the sideshow that Judy Moran's life has become continues. In October 2009, she used a friend to approach the press with a list of grievances about the conditions she was being held under in the Dame Phyllis Frost Centre, including the fact that she was not able to get her leukaemia medicine.

A former veteran police detective was reported as saying he felt no sympathy for Mrs Moran, a woman known for her love of the good life.

'At the end of the day, there's no designer cells,' he said to newspapers.

Not long after in November, Court documents were lodged alleging the division of gangland patriarch Lewis Moran's estate after his 2004 death had sparked a rift between his widow and his brother, with Judy purportedly feeling she deserved more than she got and would thus benefit by getting rid of her brother-in-law. This confirmed rumours that had been floating around insinuating such.

And then, in what has to be one of the

...'concerned about the sinister aspect of serving the charge of murder'.

strangest twists of all, indeed 'stranger than fiction' or in fact like something from an episode of the perennial Australian prison drama *Prisoner*, occurred in January 2010.

Sources at the Dame Phyllis Frost Centre confirmed Judy had a confrontation with Tania Herman, serving time for her part in the 'woman-in-the boot' murder of Maria Korp. The fight was over who would be 'top dog' and, unfortunately for the older matriarch, she lost.

Newspapers reported that their source believed,

'Judy was getting too big for her boots. She whinges like a stuck pig and was carrying on like she's the queen…Herman put her back in her box. They call her "Muscles" in there, you know.'

Prison sources went on to confirm that there had indeed been a confrontation.

'There was no punches or anything, but Judy knew where she stood after it,' a source said.

It is believed Judy was something of a target because of her notoriety, and that other inmates had tried to intimidate her. A spokesman for Corrections Victoria denied claims of a turf war in the Centre.

'Victoria has not received any complaints and is not aware of any incidents,' the spokes-

> **'Judy was getting too big for her boots. She whinges like a stuck pig and was carrying on like she's the queen…**

man said.

The screw turned another notch in possibly the final twist in the saga for Judy Moran on 18 January 2010.

During a bail application for Suzanne Kane, Prosecutor Geoff Horgan SC revealed to the Supreme Court phone conversations from the day of 'Dezzie's' murder. Speaking in code, as she drove around near the eventual location of Tuppence' demise, Judy uttered the two words to Armour that would seal her brother-in-law's fate.

'Murder on'.

Just two words...which could ultimately seal Judy Moran's fate.

Whatever happens from here on in, it would seem that as the final chapters of the Moran Clan's colourful drama play out, at the very least, Judy's days of *Cristal* and caviar are well and truly over.

> **Judy uttered the two words to Armour that would seal her brother-in-law's fate. 'Murder on'.**

FOLLOWING HER MAN

Tony Mokbel

...forced into a globetrotting lifestyle as Mokbel attempted to outrun capture by Australian authorities

'You can't help who you fall in love with.'

Such might be the sentiments of anyone who has loved, but they ring particularly true for Danielle McGuire, de facto partner of Melbourne gangland heavyweight, Tony Mokbel, who uttered them before she flew from Australia in 2007.

This occurred not long after Mokbel had fled to escape sentencing over a major cocaine importation.

She went on to proclaim,

'I'm not an angel but I just want to keep my private life private and my business life business...I'm an adult. I've made my own choices in life and I have to live with that.'

McGuire, nearing 40, was forced into a globetrotting lifestyle as Mokbel attempted to outrun capture by Australian authorities, only to eventually be caught and, despite a massive legal fight, be extradited from Greece in 2008.

Like many who mingle with underworld identities, McGuire carries her own links with crime figures. Her mother is close friend to lifetime criminal and hit man, 63-year-old, Rodney Collins, charged with the 2004 executions of police informer Terry Hodson and his wife Christine. Collins was also recently charged with the murders of Ray and Dorothy Abbey, both shot in the back of the head execution-style in their West Heidelberg home in July 1987.

McGuire has allegedly been involved in past relationships with two other ganglands identities who found unsavoury ends. Mark Moran was murdered outside his home in Essendon in June 2000, a murder which remained unsolved and which was simply attributed to being part of the gangland wars until it was pinned on Carl Williams in 2005.

Danielle has also been linked romantically to Nik 'the Russian' Radev, shot in Coburg in April 2003, with police believing Andrew Veniamin and, once again, Carl Williams, being behind the killing.

The former hairdresser has a 14-year-old daughter from a previous relationship and in recent years she and Mokbel became the parents of a girl they named Renate, after his sister-in-law. The four shared a fugitive existence in Athens while Tony was on the run. McGuire and her two daughters were abroad for two years, returning to Australia shortly after Mokbel was extradited to Australia from his Athens jail.

Although recently cleared of the charge of murdering drug dealer Michael Marshall, Mokbel still faces charges over the slaying of

McGuire has allegedly been involved in past relationships with two other ganglands identities...

Lewis Moran and others.

When Danielle McGuire originally left Australia she was noted as stating,

'I'd rather Tony was out there somewhere, than sitting in a cell.'

This forlorn wish for her man appears to be a rapidly fading hope.

'I'd rather Tony was out there somewhere, than sitting in a cell.'

Danielle McGuire and daughter

ZARAH GARDE-WILSON

Despite the fact that many women say they love 'a bad boy', it is still inconceivable that an attractive, well-educated, intelligent young woman could fall in love with a poorly educated man who was a habitual criminal and convicted murderer.

Zarah Garde-Wilson

Following such a man's predictably violent death, it is even more perplexing that she continues to be a 'serial offender' in her choice of dubious partners. Rather than a 'battered-wife' syndrome, she appears to be hexed with some strange 'gangland-man' affliction.

Zarah Garde-Wilson graduated in Law from a Perth University, going on to establish a busy law firm in Melbourne. In many of her cases she has acted in court for underworld figures such as Sean Sonnet, Roberta Williams and Tony Mokbel. She allegedly became involved in a brief affair with Mokbel and remains friendly with Williams.

After acting as defence counsel for convicted murderer Lewis Caine, she became his mistress and the pair lived together in a city apartment. Garde-Wilson conveniently ignored the fact that Caine had battered another man to death when she lovingly described him as being 'the most incredible man to walk the earth.' After other gangsters gunned him down in a

Garde-Wilson conveniently ignored the fact that Caine had battered another man to death...

Brunswick lane in 2004, she was devastated, but found comfort in the belief that his death was decided by 'karma'—that it was a pre-destined outcome. At the time, Garde-Wilson maintained Caine and she shared a deep spiritual love that continued beyond the grave.

At one point, Garde-Wilson had her certificate to practice law removed by the Victorian Legal Services Board (this was later restored and she continues to practice today, although the contempt charge was upheld). This occurred after she refused to provide evidence against Keith Faure and Evangelos Goussis, the two men who faced trial for the murder of Lewis Caine. She maintained she was too frightened to testify against Faure because he issued death threats against her before the trial began. Both men were subsequently found guilty of Caine's murder, despite the lack of any evidence from Garde-Wilson, and she was cleared to practise again as of mid 2008.

...she was too frightened to testify against Faure because he issued death threats against her before the trial began...

The glamorous Melbourne lawyer, now aged 32, continues to attract controversial headlines. She has been known to drape a python around her neck before greeting visiting police officers to her office premises and has also been photographed in sexy and revealing poses for various magazine publications.

On 13 June 2008, her most recent lover, to who she was pregnant, Lansley 'Lance'

Simon, was charged with ruining nine expensive handbags at the exclusive Southbank Versace boutique. Simon was remanded in custody after he liberally spattered the handbags with spray paint.

While visiting him at Barwon Prison, Garde-Wilson's vehicle was detected carrying significant drug equipment supplies. It was alleged 125 syringes were found in the boot, which she claimed were for her boyfriend, who allegedly used them to inject legal steroids.

Simon pleaded guilty in March 2009, paid the store for the damaged goods, apologised for his actions and was ordered to do community service.

With Simon as her latest lover, it would seem that Wilson-Garde continues to attract men who are trouble. One would hazard a guess that if ever her relationship with him goes off the rails, given her track record so far, it looks as though she might end up with another lover of similar shady background.

...125 syringes were found in the boot, which she claimed were for her boyfriend...

SECTION SEVEN

PUSHED TO THE LIMIT: MASS MURDERERS

*I'm not your executioner. I'm not your devil
and I'm not your God. I'm Charles Manson*

Charles Manson

It is highly unusual to link mass murderers with the concept of a crime of passion.

Yet, occasionally there is something about the nature and motivation behind the killing spree these insane murderers go on that contains elements associated with crimes of passion.

Australia has escaped relatively unscathed, when compared to other countries (and notably the USA) from some of the mass murder atrocities other nations have had to deal with.

This is not to say, however, that we have remained totally untouched by such tragedies and, in fact, can lay infamous claim to one of the worst mass murders the world has seen in recent times.

AUSTRALIA'S OWN 'CHARLES MANSON'

Archie McCafferty

...he was hearing voices which ordered him to kill seven people as revenge for his son's demise.

During the late 1960s, the killing sprees in America of Charles Manson and his 'family' shocked most Australians and people from all over the world.

A decade later, our own 'magnet of evil' gathered a group of thugs around him who would go on to inflict indiscriminate violence in Sydney.

During his formative years in Australia's largest city, Scottish born Archie McCafferty was involved in petty crime, but appeared to become more settled after he married and fathered a child.

This scenario drastically changed when in tragic circumstances six-week old Craig McCafferty died from suffocation after his mother fell asleep while breast-feeding and fell on top of the infant.

Following his son's sudden death, Archie McCafferty received psychiatric care. At the conclusion of his treatment, the bitter man threatened family members who he blamed for Craig's death.

Furthermore, McCafferty believed he was hearing voices which ordered him to kill seven people as revenge for his son's demise. Clearly, the unfortunate demise of his son had damaged him irrevocably and he now felt a deep-abiding passion to somehow seek vengeance.

Before long, the persuasive McCafferty had gathered a young group of individuals around him who slavishly followed his commands—his girlfriend, Carol Howes; 16-year-old psychiatric patient, Julie Todd; and teen-agers Richard Whittington, Michael Meredith and Rick Webster. Under his influence, they indulged in heroin and Angel Dust, which no doubt fuelled the rampage of terror they later went on.

Their first victim was aging war veteran, George Anson.

The gang robbed and killed him, with McCafferty especially brutal, kicking and stabbing the old man repeatedly, even after he lapsed into unconsciousness. Rick Webster later questioned his leader about the ferocity of the attack and the heavily tattooed Scot replied that he objected to Anson swearing at him.

Three nights later, during a graveside visit to his deceased son in Leppington Cemetery, Todd and Meredith joined the other gang members with a hostage. The captive was 42-year-old Ronald Cox who had innocently picked the pair up as hitchhikers. Despite his pleas for mercy, the luckless father of seven died after McCafferty shot him in the back

...the luckless father of seven died after McCafferty shot him in the back of the head.

of the head.

Two down…five to go.

And so, the killing agenda continued. The gang's hypnotic leader ordered them to find another five victims so that he could reach the mystical target of seven. Three hours after Cox's death, another hitchhiking expedition netted the group a young driving instructor, Evangelos Kollias.

Kollias was abducted and taken to McCafferty's unit, where Whittington shot him twice in the head. The corpse was unceremoniously dumped in the street.

The corpse was unceremoniously dumped in the street.

The next three targets were Archie McCafferty's mother, wife and fellow gang member Rick Webster, who had fallen from grace after criticising his leader's disturbing behaviour. Becoming aware of the plot, the frightened young man phoned police after he watched gang members gather outside the offices of the Sydney Morning Herald where he worked as a compositor.

Armed police arrested the group and their leader, labelled as 'Mad Dog', charging each member with three counts of murder.

At the subsequent trial, McCafferty pleaded insanity resulting from the death of his baby son. He told the court his son had spoken to him in a dream, telling him that if he killed seven people he would be reincarnated.

'I think, if given the chance, I will kill again for the simple reason that I have to kill seven people and I have killed only three, which means I have four to go,' he proclaimed in a clearly damning statement.

The jury rejected the insanity plea and Archie McCafferty received a life sentence. Meredith and Whittington were sentenced to 18 years in custody, while Todd and Webster received ten years and four years respectively. Howes, expecting McCafferty's child, was found not guilty.

McCafferty proved to be a serial nuisance in custody. His dangerous behaviour saw him regularly transferred within the prison system where his evil mission to kill another four to reach his magic total of seven was partially met. In 1981, a further 14 years were added to his sentence after he was convicted of the manslaughter of a fellow prisoner.

To the dismay of British authorities, he was unexpectedly paroled and deported to the UK in 1997. Back in Scotland, McCafferty drifted from home to home in Glasgow and Edinburgh. A year later, he was put on two years' probation for threatening to kill two policemen in Edinburgh.

He fled to New Zealand not long after, but in 2002 was deported back to the UK for failing to declare his criminal convictions

...14 years were added to his sentence after he was convicted of the manslaughter of a fellow prisoner.

to New Zealand immigration authorities. In 2004, at the age of 54, he was charged with the attempted murder of his 36-year-old wife Mandy after a fight broke out and he slashed her arm with a knife. She fled the unit with their youngest child, Chloe, leaving McCafferty holding their other child, a five-year-old boy, at knifepoint.

After this, it would appear Mad Dog calmed down, changing his name to James Lok and starting up a relationship with yet again a much younger woman. In late 2008, he was given 200 hours of community service for resetting a car in the same year his partner, 32-year-old Sandra Morgan, had her children taken into care when it was discovered she was dating the convicted killer, despite him having no contact with them.

...will he kill the remaining three to lay his son's soul to rest?

The question remains, however, does Mad Dog still hear the voices, and will he kill the remaining three to lay his son's soul to rest?

MARTIN BRYANT

Some might argue that Martin Bryant's twisted soul was pushed into the heinous crimes he committed due to the passion he felt for his family—the desire to protect their interests, albeit a the most extreme way that no sane person would.

Martin Bryant

On 28 April 1996, Bryant became the most notorious mass murderer in Australian history, and indeed ranked in the top 10 worldwide in terms of sheer number of victims. On that pleasant autumn Sunday afternoon at the peaceful Tasmanian tourist resort of Port Arthur, Bryant murdered 35 people and injured 18 others before armed police ended the horrendous slaughter.

Prior to that fateful day, Bryant had been regularly dismissed by most who knew him as merely an eccentric, slightly irritating loner. And yet year's later, psychologists who have studied his case would argue that he in no way displayed any real 'major alert' signs to indicate he was about to embark on such a massive killing spree.

During his childhood, a young Martin was seen as dull and spiteful, shunned by his peers. His IQ of 66 meant he was functioning intellectually in the lowest one to two per cent of the population, but his parents mistakenly

...Bryant murdered 35 people and injured 18 others before armed police ended the horrendous slaughter.

sent him to a mainstream school. Throughout those bleak years, the tall blonde-headed boy with a mental age far below his actual became the object of scorn and derision. According to psychological reports, his memories of school were unpleasant and distressing, and he recalled frequently being bullied and having few, if any, friends.

At the completion of his unhappy school-days, given his poor literary and numeracy skills, Bryant never held down any permanent work. His father, Maurice, attempted to compensate for his son's limitations. The conscientious parent gave up his former job and attempted to form a market gardening business with his offspring. The emotional strain proved too much for him and, two years before the Port Arthur massacre, Maurice Bryant took his own life.

...two years before the Port Arthur massacre, Maurice Bryant took his own life.

This tragedy appeared to weigh heavily on Martin, and it would ultimately be one of the tipping points that pushed him over the edge to commit the crimes at Port Arthur.

His father was one of only two people who truly seemed to care for him. The other was Helen Harvey, an eccentric middle-aged heiress, with who Martin shared a close and allegedly platonic friendship. She originally employed him as a handyman, but the young man's good looks and extremely blonde hair possibly resulted in him becoming something of a child substitute for the lonely spinster.

When Harvey died in a car accident, Martin inherited the six-figure fortune she left behind. The desperately lonely young man used his sudden wealth to finance companionship on long international plane trips. Pleasure or education were not the driving motivations behind his frequent flying episodes—Bryant valued more the opportunity to converse with any person who became an unlucky captive audience once they were allocated a seat next to him on long flights.

Although his inheritance was placed in the hands of the Perpetual Trustees of Tasmania as a means of protecting it from being misused by him in his impaired intellectual state, what he did gain access to he spent on accumulating a large teddy bear collection (up to 200) and a selection of violent videos. Significantly, just before the killing spree began, his mother Carleen, with whom he never shared a close relationship, became worried about his moody behaviour. Her instincts were well-founded as her son was secretly amassing an arsenal of deadly weapons.

...her son was secretly amassing an arsenal of deadly weapons.

Two sets of handcuffs, a supply of sashcord rope, a hunting knife and several canisters of petrol were all carefully packed into his yellow Volvo by 8am on the day the multiple

Bryant carried three semi-automatic weapons, and huge supplies of ammunition...

killings were planned for, and his sports bag contained dangerous combat guns. With him, Bryant carried three semi-automatic weapons, and huge supplies of ammunition were at the ready for the mass slaughter that lay ahead.

Ironically, Bryant's program of revenge against a society that had consistently rejected him for over 20 years was enacted when life seemed to have improved considerably for the disturbed young man. He had found the security and companionship he craved in a relationship with Petra Wilmott, spending the night with her before embarking on his killing spree.

In their book, *Born or Bred? The Making of a Mass Murderer* published in 2009, Robert Wainwright and Paola Totaro provide some interesting possibilities about Martin Bryant's mindset on the day the massacre occurred. The writers suggest he was nearly diverted from carrying out his obsessive and deadly plan and there can be no doubt that there are aspects of Martin Bryant's behaviour on the morning of 28 April 1996 which indicate he may have had second thoughts about his crazed mission.

On his short journey to Port Arthur, Bryant made numerous irrelevant stops. He purchased a bottle of tomato sauce for no apparent reason, bought a cigarette lighter (even though he was a non-smoker), had a coffee break when he attempted to start a conversation about surfing, and topped up his car with petrol. Wainwright and Totaro raise the possibility that this series of random stops was Bryant procrastinating. Was he giving a world, which had consistently dismissed him, one last chance to show respect and friendship?

The authors go on to suggest that perhaps if just one of the people Bryant buttonholed that morning had treated him in a more compassionate and worthwhile way, the terror that was to become the Port Arthur massacre may not have occurred?

Overall, however, despite his personal demons, the shooting spree Martin Bryant engaged in was almost impossible for others to predict.

It was difficult for the socially inept 28-year-old to curb an obsessive grudge that had developed following the death of his father two years previously. Before Maurice Bryant's suicide, he had attempted to buy the nearby Seascape Guesthouse. However, David and Noelene Martin became the owners, something Martin Bryant bitterly resented as a setback to his family and which he believed was done as a spiteful and intentional act to prevent his father from owning it. Bryant construed from this that they were therefore directly responsible for his father taking his own life and the

Bryant construed from this that they were therefore directly responsible for his father taking his own life...

ultimate downfall of his family.

Sadly, for the Bryant family, Martin's ideas were compounded by the fact that his father had bitterly complained at the time of the lost opportunity that they had been double-crossed by the successful bidders for the property—a myth which would be perpetuated by the family.

In light of this, the Martins became the first and possibly the main targets for Bryant's day of Armageddon. Once the elderly couple were disposed of, he continued a series of random executions. His next 'death-stop' was another guesthouse in which his late father had shown interest. Fortunately, the owners were out and thus their lives were spared.

Once the elderly couple were disposed of, he continued a series of random executions.

Bryant moved on to the tranquil Port Arthur site where he complained to a parking attendant that another patron had nearly backed into him. He then ignored directions from the polite official and drove his Volvo into a prohibited area before walking to the Broad Arrow Café.

There, while having a snack on the outside deck near the main dining area, Bryant muttered mostly incoherent statements about 'wasps' whenever Asian visitors were near, and at approximately 1.30 pm entered the area where many tourists were eating. Producing an AR-15 semi-automatic rifle from his sports bag, he rapidly fired off 29 rounds of ammunition, killing 22 unsuspecting diners in one hit.

Some sceptics challenge the belief that Martin Bryant acted independently in this initial shooting rampage, claiming it was almost impossible for Bryant to target so many 'head shots' accurately when he was holding the weapon against his hip and firing indiscriminately. These theorists maintain that at least one other assailant must have assisted Bryant in the massacre, although there is little other evidence to support such.

Following the initial carnage, the remorseless killer moved back to the car park where he continued to murder tourists at random. A short stop at his Volvo saw him change his weapon for a TNS2RT7.62 mm rifle which he used to shoot a coach driver, fatally, and to inflict serious wounds on others.

Bryant then committed what many consider the most callous murders of that horrendous afternoon.

As he walked back to his car, he spotted Nanette Mikac with her two daughters. Without hesitation, he first shot dead the mother and then her three-year-old, Madeline, before chasing down and slaying six-year-old Alanah.

The next four homicide cases were occu-

Following the initial carnage, the remorseless killer moved back to the car park where he continued to murder tourists at random.

The woman was shot dead and the man was forced at gunpoint into the boot of the BMW.

pants of a gold BMW sedan, which the killer procured and drove back towards the Seascape Guesthouse. On the way, he confronted two occupants of a white Toyota. The woman was shot dead and the man was forced at gunpoint into the boot of the BMW. Bryant's hostage was then handcuffed to a rail near the guesthouse. He was later killed, possibly in crossfire exchanges between the mass murderer and police expert shooters.

Police began firing at Bryant in the guesthouse around 4pm, beginning an 18-hour siege. Phone contact was established with him during the armed standoff and the defiant young man referred to himself as 'Jamie' when demanding a ride in a police helicopter.

The next morning, in an apparent suicide attempt, Bryant set fire to the guesthouse and was arrested when, with his clothes alight, he dashed from the burning building. As paramedics attempted to treat his burns, Bryant angrily accused them of deliberately applying petrol to them.

When Martin Bryant later faced court for multiple murder charges via a video link from prison, he displayed no empathy towards his 35 victims. Rather, he appeared to enjoy his notoriety as he smiled and giggled during proceedings. He was found guilty on all counts and his 35 life sentences effectively mean he will never be released from Hobart's Risdon Prison. Recent accounts suggest that in custody, Martin Bryant has become an obese shell-of-a-person. He has attempted suicide at least six times and now communicates with no one.

Federal and State governments introduced tougher new gun laws in the wake of the Port Arthur massacre. Ownership rules were tightened; a range of weapons were outlawed, bought back from previous owners and destroyed by government agencies; and bans were placed on most military-style automatic weapons.

Walter Mikac, the husband of the late Nanette, and father of two slain daughters, became a prominent anti-gun lobbyist after the tragedy and his strong advocacy helped bring about significant changes. Former Prime Minister, John Howard, was also active in promoting much-needed reform. Today in Australia, gun ownership has become more dependent on need, compared to the past where it was often an accepted practice for any adults in most communities.

In the now restful environment of Port Arthur, a new restaurant has been built and a memorial garden established.

He has attempted suicide at least six times and now communicates with no one.

INDEX

BIBLIOGRAPHY

The Age newspaper (various)

The Sunday Age newspaper (various)

The Herald Sun newspaper (various)

The NLA Australian Newspapers archive

Engel, Howard, *Crimes of Passion*, Anova Books, 2004

Ferguson, Ian, *Crimes that shocked Australia*, Brolga Publishing, 2008

Ferguson, Ian, *Murders that Shocked Australia*, Brolga Publishing, 2007

More great titles from the Brolga true crime series

Murders that shocked Australia
by Ian Ferguson
ISBN 9781921221538 $24.95

The second edition of this best-seller takes the reader through Australia's most challenging murders and personalities, from Ned Kelly to the baffling Pyjama Girl case. Enthralling and chilling, Ian Ferguson explores the true-life cases that have gripped Australia and our media.

Prison Break
by Joe Tog
ISBN 9781921221583 $24.95

Isolated in a small cell in Brisbane's maximum-security prison, Joe Tog composed a series of short narratives for his defence-barrister. Chronicling the events leading up to his arrest in far-north Queensland, *Prison Break* tells the true story of a man who has lived to tell the tale of breaking out of Australian prison – more than once.

Raw Deal
by Wayne McKay
ISBN 9781921221484 $24.95

Raw Deal is the amazing story of an ex-con who turned his life around. Detailing life on the street, in jail and without friends or family, this is one man's tale of how a life of hardship, brutality and little hope can be turned around. A story you have to read to believe.

Order your copies

		Qty
Crimes of Passion that Shocked Australia	AU$24.99	.....
Prison Break	AU$24.99	.....
Raw Deal	AU$19.99	.....
Murders that Shocked Australia	AU$19.99	.....
Crimes that Shocked Australia	AU$19.99	.....
Postage within Australia (1–2 books)	AU$6.00	.....
Postage within Australia (3+ books)	AU$12.00	.....

TOTAL* $_____

* All prices include GST

Name: ....

Address: ....

Phone: ....

Email Address: ....

Payment: ❏ Money Order ❏ Cheque ❏ Amex ❏ MasterCard ❏ Visa

Cardholder's Name: ....

Credit Card Number: ....

Signature: ....

Expiry Date: ....

Allow 21 days for delivery.

Payment to: Better Bookshop (ABN 14 067 257 390)
              PO Box 12544
              A'Beckett Street, Melbourne, 8006
              Victoria, Australia
              sales@brolgapublishing.com.au

BE PUBLISHED

Publishing through a successful Australian publisher.
Brolga provides:
  • Editorial appraisal
  • Cover design
  • Typesetting
  • Printing
  • Author promotion
  • National book trade distribution, including
sales, marketing and distribution through
Macmillan Australia.

For details and inquiries, contact:

Brolga Publishing Pty Ltd
PO Box 12544
A'Beckett St VIC 8006
Ph: +61 3 9600 4982
bepublished@brolgapublishing.com.au
markzocchi@brolgapublishing.com.au
ABN: 46 063 962 443